About This Issue

The cover of this edition of *eJournal USA* captures a Russian woman's horror as she gazes at photographs of children killed in the terrorist attack on a school in Beslan, Russia, in 2004. Some 330 people, more than half of them children, died when Chechen terrorists in opposition to the Russian government took more than 1,200 hostages by seizing the school and wiring it to explode.

The woman's face registers a universal response to such horrific mass violence—anguish, shock, incomprehension. As John Horgan, of St. Andrews University's Centre for the Study of Terrorism and Political Violence, writes in this issue, the most common reaction to terrorist atrocities is baffled revulsion: "How could anyone do this?" And, of course, there is a second question to ask: What can be done to thwart the networks that recruit those who become terrorists and perform such acts?

To provide some answers to these questions and take a comprehensive look at the complex, global problem of terrorism, the editors of *eJournal USA* invited many of the world's leading scholars in this field to examine the motivations of those who carry out terrorist attacks and the techniques that terrorist organizations such as al-Qaida use to recruit and motivate them.

In our opening interview, award-winning filmmaker Sharmeen Obaid-Chinoy describes the effects of terrorism on Afghan child refugees. Other essays put the phenomenon in a historical context, examine how terrorists are psychologically able to justify the killing of innocents, and delineate how they use the media and theatrical techniques to manipulate the public and spread their message. Several case studies analyze the recruitment of suicide bombers in Iraq and profile women who become terrorists. We conclude with an article by Australian counterterrorism expert David Kilcullen, who identifies terrorism as a new kind of threat, one that requires new paradigms for developing strategies to combat it.

It is only by understanding the terrorist mentality that civil societies can hope to counter terrorist tactics effectively.

— The Editors

U.S. DEPARTMENT OF STATE / MAY 2007 / VOLUME 12 / NUMBER 5

http://usinfo.state.gov/pub/ejournalusa.html

Countering the Terrorist Mentality

Online Video

Terrorism: A War Without Borders
(Source: U.S. Department of State)

*http://usinfo.state.gov/journals/itps/0507/ijpe/
ijpe0507.htm*

Terrorism and Children

An Interview With Sharmeen Obaid-Chinoy

Sharmeen Obaid-Chinoy, a journalist and film producer, has won many international awards for her documentaries and is the first non-American to be awarded the prestigious Livingston Award, a U.S. reporting prize for media professionals under the age of 35. She holds masters degrees in both international policy studies and communications from Stanford University in California.

Q: Your film *Children of Terror* focused on young Afghan refugees in your home country of Pakistan. Why did you choose them as a documentary topic?

A: I spent 10 weeks living with these children in a refugee camp in Karachi and realized very early on that their experiences were quite different from that of most children in Pakistan. It was clear that these children have been greatly affected by the violence they have grown up with, and that will influence the type of adults they become. I felt that their story needed to be told.

Q: What can you tell us about the cumulative losses children experience in societies where family and civil structures have been overwhelmed by terrorist violence?

A: Terrorism intentionally creates insecurity and fear. It deliberately ruins the social fabric of a society by ignoring the common laws of humanity—then many of those with education or financial means flee, and those who remain try to live amid the violence and downward economic spiral. Families are destroyed and children are robbed of their innocence. The losses they experience are material, social, and emotional.

Having grown up amid violence, the young boys I came to know in the camp were more familiar with Kalishnikovs and APC guns than they were with their alphabet. They spoke about the fear they felt—at night when they could not sleep because of bomb blasts and gunfire, about being injured when outside of their home in the daytime, and about being forcibly recruited into or confronted by a local militia.

When a generation grows up under this kind of

Photo Removed Due to Copyright Restrictions

©2007 SharmeenObaidfilms.com

One unfortunate effect of terrorism is to force children to take on adult responsibilities, such as becoming the financial provider for their families. These Afghan boys found work as child laborers weaving rugs in Pakistan.

violence and fear, it is deprived of an education and knowledge of its true culture. Young children are forced to fend for themselves on the streets—often sent out to scavenge for food or to work at dangerous jobs for money. They are treated as adults and not as children. This is one of the successes of the perpetrators of random violence: They create an environment where children cannot behave as children but, instead, are forced to take on adult responsibilities.

Most of the young boys I spoke with had never spent much time with their fathers or older brothers because they, the adult males, had either been killed or were away from home for a long time. These young boys were essentially, then, the "men" about the house, handed the responsibility of providing for and protecting the women of the family. They had to learn how to use a gun at the age of six or seven and, by the time they were 14 or 15, were ready to go off to fight themselves.

This is how terrorists ensure having a steady supply of recruits—creating an unworkable society, then offering an alternative one—one which they, of course, control with violence, intimidation, and manipulation. They make use of disasters, both natural ones and those they created, by offering aid to those in need, but with very tangled strings attached.

Q: How does recruitment take place?

A: Children are the perfect recruits for terrorists because they do not have the ability to question adult motives, are easily swayed by appeals to their emotions, and can be readily convinced to undertake whatever job is asked of them.

Decades before "jihad" began in the Muslim world, child soldiers were being recruited in Africa and in South America. In those wars, children proved to be fearless. After all, study after study tells us that the young are impulsive and inclined toward taking risks. They are too developmentally immature to properly judge their ability to handle situations or see the potentials for tragedy.

Every parent knows that children, oblivious to how their actions can affect themselves and others, often make poor decisions. That is why children can and have been repeatedly exploited by others. That is also precisely why children need to be educated, to be able to reflect on matters, consider consequences, and develop understanding.

In the Muslim world, many children are being manipulated simply by being forced onto the street. They have to find food and money however they can. If they are boys, they might be offered a place in a religious school where they will be fed and taught—but what they are taught may be a fundamentalist ideology that is intolerant of others, and even intolerant of those who practice the same religion but differently, that sees the West and its ways as an enemy to be conquered.

These children are being cajoled or coerced into joining jihad and are recruited precisely because their very youth can be exploited: Not immediately recognized as a threat, they can slip in and out of highly secure areas while playing football on the streets. They are the perfect foil for terrorists—so naïve they do not have a clear idea of what is expected of them until it is too late.

Contrary to what the West may think, terrorists are becoming more successful in their recruitment of young Muslim men and, even more troubling, young women to their cause. One of the biggest reasons for this victory is their success in keeping much of the Islamic world poorly educated and closed to new ideas.

Q: What about the parents of these children?

A: The reaction of parents can be surprising. Poverty and illiteracy play a major role in determining their beliefs. In Southern Afghanistan, many of the families I spoke with were proud of the fact that their young sons—some less than 15 years old—had glorified the name of Islam by "attacking the enemy." These particular young boys belonged to large families; some had up to 10 siblings. Their parents were poor and could not take care of them, so they had been sent off to remote Islamic schools in Pakistan. Their parents barely knew them anymore.

As I pointed out earlier, many of the adult males are gone, and often the women and their daughters, already denied education, are forbidden to work outside the home. If given a choice between school, food, and clothing or sorting through garbage for sustenance, ... well, sometimes there is no choice.

That is one of the reasons that terrorists are so successful in convincing young boys to join them and adopt their point of view, because they do not have a

Photo Removed Due to Copyright Restrictions

©AP Images/Karel Prinsloo
These young soldiers from a Congolese rebel movement group are among the hundreds of thousands of children under the age of 18 who are recruited to fight worldwide.

Photo Removed Due to Copyright Restrictions

Teacher in Pakistan school linked to al-Qaida.

support system to fall back upon or parents to confer with; they are often under severe peer pressure to sign up, to belong to something that is more organized than the streets, for a chance to attain some kind of glory or redeem their honor.

At the same time, poor parents collect economic rewards for the sacrifice of their sons and daughters to suicide terrorism and receive selected passages from the Quran—without any proper context—which show that their children died following the instructions of the Prophet. Solitary women, especially, sometimes gain a distinctive social status in the community, aside from monetary support, for being the mother of martyrs.

The attitude toward women and education, the poverty, constant violence, and fear … it all makes for a very complicated situation.

Q: Tell us a little about some of the children in your film—in particular, the serious boy who accompanied you to the public swimming pool, the gentle one who worked in the rug factory, and the bright and sparkling little girl who did not want to get married.

A: Khal Mohammed was 11 and, without family in the camp, had been taken into a fundamentalist school. Although he could not read, he memorized all the verses of the Quran, an enormous accomplishment. He was a very stern boy, however, and when we went to the public swimming pool, where the women were fully covered—except for their faces, hands, and feet—he insisted that not only were they "bad" but that he would go to hell for having even been among these people acting "immorally" in their holiday enjoyment.

Noor Mohammed was 10 and solely responsible for financially supporting his family by doing the dangerous and difficult work of making rugs. Another intelligent child, he spoke wistfully of his life before his father and uncle were killed and how he would be in school if they were still alive. During the making of our film, he lost his job for being late for work—there were many boys eager to take his place—because of having to attend to his older, drug-addicted brother who was in the hospital.

Laila, also 10, repeatedly said she did not want to get married but, instead, wanted an education, while her father gently admonished her, explaining that she would shortly be betrothed because, as she got older, she needed a man to protect her. Indeed, the main game for the girls in the camp was playing "wedding."

Young girls are particularly vulnerable to recruitment to extremist ideology because few other paths are offered them. In countries like Pakistan, fundamentalist religious schools are already carefully inducting young women, realizing that by indoctrinating them, they are able to control an entire family. A woman goes home from the mosque, educates her children, and talks to her neighbors, and thus the ideology flourishes and grows. This is the first step toward militarizing women.

We are already seeing the next step. Recently in Islamabad, a group of women, wielding sticks, demanded that video shops be closed and music stores banned. They attacked a house where they felt immoral behavior was taking place and kidnapped the women living in the house. Some of these female militants sitting in judgment of others were barely 15 years old. That is the effectiveness of the proponents of fundamentalist ideology. Today, they are raiding a house against "immoral" fellow Muslims and tomorrow they may very well choose to strap on bombs and become suicide bombers against "infidels."

Indeed, many well-educated, Western-born Muslim women are susceptible to recruitment. I wrote an article that looked at Muslim religious schools in Mississauga, Canada. There, young Canadian-Muslim women are being told to shun the Western world they live in. These women, brainwashed into covering their faces and adhering to sexual segregation, are continually told that their Muslim brothers are dying in battles to defend their honor so that Western men are not able to "defile" them. Ironically, they reject the very political system that gives them the choices they currently enjoy. This is a difficult problem because in societies like Canada and the United States, where multiculturalism and freedom of religion are not only encouraged but a bedrock of societal belief, many people do not question the teachings being put forth in religious schools. It is a fundamental tenet that females have the right to an education and the right to practice the tenets of their faith. Unfortunately, these empowered women are learning a very extreme interpretation of Islam, one in direct conflict with the society they grew up in and against which they, and their children, are bound to clash in the future.

Q: What do you believe is the future for these children?

A: It is estimated that more than 50 percent of the world's Muslim population is under the age of 18, which is a terrifying demographic, especially since most of these young people have little or no access to education and employment. They are frustrated by the corrupt governments that rule them. They see double standards played out by the West, which insists on democracy in Iraq, but not elsewhere in the region. They are aware that Islam was once the foundation of a great culture, and they wonder what has happened because their generation has experienced only poverty, war and destruction, corruption, and nepotism. Somehow, this problem must be turned to an advantage: These young people, if properly educated and given opportunity, could instead be the engine of change and economic progress.

True Islam encourages Muslims to adapt to changing times, but extreme fundamentalists have always opposed anything new, from the telegraph to television. They oppose modern education because they say that it teaches topics that are not in harmony with Islam. Educated Muslims know that this is a ploy to prevent young, active minds from challenging them.

It becomes a vicious cycle: By deliberately depriving young Muslims from receiving a good education, the fundamentalists ensure that the future of their potential recruits is bleak and the resulting frustrations make them easily susceptible to terrorist ideology. That ideology requires them to violently reject any ideas that challenge fundamentalist precepts and prevents their learning the importance of freedom of thought and speech that separate logical ideas from emotional biases, the very thing on which the vibrant societies that most people want for their children can be built. ∎

The opinions expressed in this article do not necessarily reflect the views or policies of the U.S. government.

Photo Removed Due to Copyright Restrictions

Afghan students from a religious school in Pakistan at a rally in Karachi, Pakistan, in 2001.

A Form of Psychological Warfare

Bruce Hoffman

Bruce Hoffman, PhD, is a professor at Georgetown University's Edmund A. Walsh School of Foreign Service and a senior fellow at the Combating Terrorism Center, U.S. Military Academy at West Point. This article is based in part on material previously published in the author's Inside Terrorism, *2nd edition (New York: Columbia University Press, 2006).*

Terrorism is the deliberate creation and exploitation of fear in the attainment of political change. It is thus undeniably a form of psychological warfare. Although people often are tragically killed and wounded by terrorists in their attacks, terrorism by its nature is designed to have far-reaching psychological effects beyond the immediate victim(s) or object of their violence. It is meant to instill fear within and thereby intimidate or otherwise affect the behavior of the terrorists' target audience.

This intended audience varies depending on the terrorists' aims, motivations, and objectives. It may include a national government or political party, a rival ethnic or religious group, an entire country and its citizens, or international opinion. The terrorist attack may either have a particular audience segment specifically in mind, or be designed to appeal to multiple audiences.

The publicity generated by a terrorist attack and the attention focused on the perpetrators are designed to create power for the terrorists, fostering an environment of fear and intimidation amenable to terrorist manipulation. In this respect, terrorism's success is best measured not by the accepted metrics of conventional warfare—number of enemy killed in battle, amount of military assets destroyed, or geographical territory seized—but rather by its ability to attract attention to the terrorists and their cause and by the psychological impact and deleterious effects that terrorists hope to exert over their target audience(s).

Terrorists use violence—or, equally important, wield the threat of violence—because they believe that only through brutal mayhem can their cause triumph and long-term political aims be attained. Operations are therefore deliberately planned to shock, impress, and intimidate—

Photo Removed Due to Copyright Restrictions

A security guard checks an Indonesian woman's bag at a Jakarta shopping mall in August 2003, following a bombing at Jakarta's Marriott Hotel that killed 13 people and injured almost 149.

ensuring that their acts are sufficiently daring and bloody enough to capture the attention of the media and, in turn, the public and government as well. Thus, rather than being seen as indiscriminate or senseless, terrorism is actually a very deliberate and planned application of violence.

What Terrorists Want

Although the aims and motivations of different types of terrorists—left and right wing, ethno-nationalist and religious, single issue and broadly utopian—may differ, they all want maximum publicity to be generated by their actions and, therefore, through intimidation and subjection, attain their objectives.

Photo Removed Due to Copyright Restrictions

Following an October 2005 warning of a terrorist threat reportedly aimed at the New York City subway, a portion of the waiting area at Penn Station is closed by police while they investigate a suspicious package.

A terrorist act is conceived and executed in a manner that simultaneously reflects the terrorist group's particular aims and motivations, fits its resources and capabilities, and takes into account the intended audience. The tactics and targets of various terrorist movements, as well as the weapons they favor, are inevitably shaped by a group's ideology, its internal organizational dynamics, the personalities of its leadership, and a variety of other internal and external stimuli. For example, 1970s-era left-wing terrorists such as West Germany's Red Army Faction and Italy's Red Brigades selectively kidnapped and assassinated specific persons, whom they blamed for economic exploitation or political repression, in order to attract publicity and promote a Marxist-Leninist revolution. Contemporary terrorists, motivated by a religious imperative, have engaged in more indiscriminate acts of violence against a far wider category of targets, encompassing not merely their declared enemies but

anyone who does not share their religious faith, and even persons who are of the same faith but who do not share the terrorists' extreme political views and theological constructs.

Terrorism, therefore, may be seen not only as a violent act deliberately conceived to attract attention but, through the publicity it generates, to communicate a message. In the words of the late Dr. Frederick Hacker, a psychiatrist and noted authority on terrorism, terrorists seek to "frighten and, by frightening, to dominate and control. They want to impress. They play to and for an audience and solicit audience participation."[1]

The death and destruction wrought by terrorism is deliberately designed to inculcate fear and adversely affect normal, daily life by threatening personal safety, thereby tearing at the social fabric of a country by destroying its business and cultural life and the mutual trust upon which society is based. Refusals to visit shopping malls, to attend sporting events, to go to the theater, movies, and concerts, or to travel abroad or within one's own country are common responses to the fear (known as "vicarious victimization") generated by the uncertainty of where and when the next terrorist attack will occur.

Terrorism and the Media

The modern news media, as the principal conduit of information about terrorism, play a vital part in the calculus. Indeed, without media coverage, the terrorists' impact is arguably wasted, remaining narrowly confined to the immediate, actual victims of the attack, rather than reaching the wider target audience. Only by spreading fear and outrage to a much larger audience can terrorists gain the maximum potential leverage they need to effect fundamental political change.

"Terrorism is theatre," Brian Jenkins famously declared in his seminal 1974 paper "International Terrorism: A New Mode of Conflict," which explains how "terrorist attacks are often carefully choreographed to attract the attention of the electronic media and the international press."[2] Just as often, the media respond to these overtures with almost unbridled eagerness, proving unable to ignore what another leading terrorism analyst, J. Bowyer Bell, accurately described as "an event ... fashioned specifically for their needs."[3]

In recent years, as a result of the Internet, terrorist media capabilities have evolved to a point where they can now control the entire communication process by determining the content, context, and medium over which their message is projected toward precisely the audience (or multiple audiences) they seek to reach.

The implications of this development are enormous, as they challenge the monopoly long exercised by commercial and state-owned broadcasting outlets over mass communication of the terrorist message. Hence, much like previous information revolutions—such as the invention of the rotary press in the mid-19th century and the advances in television equipment that made the reporting of events in real time possible in the 1960s—the new information revolution has profoundly empowered terrorist groups with the ability to shape and disseminate their own message in their own way, completely bypassing traditional, established media outlets.

The Role of the Internet

As Tina Brown, the doyenne of postmodern media, astutely observed in 2005, "[T]he conjunction of 21st-century Internet speed and 12th-century fanaticism has turned our world into a tinderbox."[4]

In addition to ubiquity and timeliness, the Internet has other advantages: It can circumvent government censorship; messages can be sent anonymously, quickly, and almost effortlessly; and it is an especially cost-effective means of mass communication.

It also enables terrorists to undertake what Professor Dorothy Denning has termed perception management[5]—portraying themselves and their actions in precisely the light and context they wish, unencumbered from the filter, screening, and spin of established media.

"It is not surprising that networked terrorists have already begun to leverage IT [information technology] for perception management and propaganda to influence public opinion, recruit new members, and generate funding," two RAND Corporation analysts have noted. "Getting a message out," they continue, "and receiving extensive news media exposure are important components of terrorist strategy, which ultimately seeks to undermine the will of an opponent. In addition to such traditional media as television or print,

Photo Removed Due to Copyright Restrictions

In this June 2003 videotape, an Arabic-speaking guerrilla claims al-Qaida responsibility for suicide bombings in Saudi Arabia and Morocco and warns of more attacks to come.

the Internet now offers terrorist groups an alternative way to reach out to the public, often with much more direct control over the message."[6]

Equally as worrisome is that the Internet, once regarded as an engine for education and enlightenment for the world, has become an essential means for the dissemination of terrorist propaganda, hate, and incitement to violence—purveying the coarsest and most base conspiracy theories with a pervasiveness that is completely divorced from reality. For instance, despite al-Qaida's own repeated claims of responsibility for the September 11, 2001, attacks and even the dissemination of "martyrdom" videotapes made by the hijackers discussing the forthcoming attacks, Web sites associated with the jihadist movement regularly post assertions that the United States or Israel carried out the attacks themselves to justify a war on terrorism that was always intended to be a "war on Islam."

The result is that the most outlandish and far-fetched views are acquiring a veneer of truth and veracity simply because of their unmitigated and unchallenged repetition and circulation throughout the Internet.

A Sanctuary for al-Qaida

Al-Qaida, in fact, is unique among other terrorist groups in all these communications respects. From its founding in the late 1980s and emergence in the early 1990s, al-Qaida's leadership seems to have intuitively grasped the enormous communicative potential of the Internet and sought to harness its power both to further the movement's strategic aims and to facilitate its tactical operations.

The priority that al-Qaida has long accorded to external communications is evidenced by its pre-9/11 organizational structure. One of the original four al-Qaida operational committees was specifically tasked with media and publicity. (The others were responsible for military operations, finance and business, and *fatwa* and Islamic study.)[7]

Egyptian computer experts, who had fought alongside al-Qaida founder and leader Osama bin Laden in Afghanistan against the Soviet Army during the 1980s, were reportedly specifically recruited to create the extensive network of Web sites, e-mail capabilities, and electronic bulletin boards that continues to function today—this despite al-Qaida's expulsion from Afghanistan, the destruction of its operational base in that country, and the ongoing prosecution of the U.S.-led global war on terrorism.

For al-Qaida, the Internet has become something of a virtual sanctuary, providing an effective, expeditious, and anonymous means to carry on communication with its fighters, followers, sympathizers, and supporters worldwide, while continuing its campaign of psychological warfare. Therefore, despite its weakened state, al-Qaida is still able to generate global fear, alarm, and anxiety.

One cannot, of course, predict what new forms and dimensions terrorism will assume during the rest of the 21st century. It is safe to say, however, that as terrorist communications continue to change and evolve, so will the nature of terrorism itself. In this respect, psychological warfare, long the mainstay of terrorist intentions and capabilities, will not only continue, but will likely be abetted and accelerated by new communications technologies—just as has been the case over the past decade. ∎

The opinions expressed in this article do not necessarily reflect the views or policies of the U.S. government.

Endnotes

1. Frederick J. Hacker, *Crusaders, Criminals, Crazies: Terror and Terrorism in Our Time* (New York: W. W. Norton, 1976), p. xi.
2. Brian Michael Jenkins, "International Terrorism: A New Mode of Conflict," in David Carlton and Carlo Schaerf (eds.), *International Terrorism and World Security* (London: Croom Helm, 1975), p. 16.
3. J. Bowyer Bell, "Terrorist Scripts and Live-action Spectaculars," *Columbia Journalism Review*, vol. 17, no. 1 (1978): p. 50.
4. Tina Brown, "Death by Error," *The Washington Post* (19 May 2005).
5. Dorothy Denning, "Information Warfare and Cyber-terrorism," Women in International Security (WIIS) Seminar, Washington, D.C. (15 December 1999).
6. Michele Zanini and Sean J.A. Edwards, "The Networking of Terror in the Information Age," in John Arquilla and David Ronfeldt (eds.), *Networks and Netwars: The Future of Terror, Crime and Militancy* (Santa Monica, CA: RAND, 2001, MR-1382-OSD), p. 43.
7. Rohan Gunaratna, *Inside Al-Qa'ida: Global Network of Terror* (London: Hurst, 2002), p. 57. The director of the media operational committee was known by the *nom de guerre* Abu Reuter—an obvious reference to the famous global news wire service.

Collective Identity: Hatred Bred in the Bone

Jerrold Post

Jerrold Post, MD, is a professor of psychiatry, political psychology, and international affairs and director of the Political Psychology Program at The George Washington University, Washington, D.C.

There is a widespread assumption that the ranks of terrorists are filled with seriously psychologically disturbed individuals. Who, after all, but a crazed fanatic, would kill innocent victims in the name of a cause, would willingly become a human bomb?

In fact, the consensus view of the committee on the psychological roots of terrorism, which I organized for the International Summit on Democracy, Terrorism, and Security held in Madrid in March 2005,[1] was that the search for individual psychopathology in understanding why people become involved in terrorism was doomed to failure, that explanations at the level of individual psychology were insufficient.

Indeed, we concluded, it is not going too far to assert that terrorists are psychologically "normal" in the sense of not being clinically psychotic. They are neither depressed nor severely emotionally disturbed, nor are they crazed fanatics. In fact, terrorist groups and organizations screen out emotionally unstable individuals—who represent, after all, a security risk.

There is a multiplicity of individual motivations. For some, it is to give a sense of power to the powerless; for others, revenge is a primary motivation; for still others, to gain a sense of significance.

Rather than individual psychology, then, what emerges as the most powerful lens through which to understand terrorist behavior is that of group, organizational, and social psychology, with a particular emphasis on "collective identity."

Collective Identity

For some groups, especially nationalist/terrorist groups, collective identity is established extremely early, so that hatred is bred in the bone. The importance of

Photo Removed Due to Copyright Restrictions

Pakistani boys hold a toy gun and an Osama bin Laden poster at a rally organized by Jamat-e-Islami (Party of Islam) in Karachi, Pakistan.

collective identities and the processes of forming and transforming them cannot be overemphasized. Terrorists have subordinated their individual identity to the collective identity, so that what serves the group, organization, or network is of primary importance.

Now, how is that collective identity shaped? Interviews with incarcerated Middle East terrorists[2] suggest that it begins very early, as evidenced by representative quotes from nationalist-separatist terrorists in Fatah and the Palestinian Front for the Liberation of Palestine:

I came from a religious family which used to observe all the Islamic traditions. My initial political awareness came during the prayers at the mosque. That's where I was also asked to join religious classes. In the context of these studies, the sheik used to inject some historical background in which he would tell us how we were effectively evicted from Palestine.

And:

The sheik used to explain to us the significance of the fact that there was an IDF [Israel Defense Forces] military outpost in the heart of the camp. He compared it to a cancer in the human body, which was threatening its very existence.

How did these terrorists justify the extremity of their actions in pursuit of their cause? One answer was especially telling:

An armed action proclaims that I am here, I exist, I am strong, I am in control, I am in the field, I am on the map.

So it is power for the powerless, significance for the insignificant. This helps explain why it is so difficult to leave the path of terrorism.

Religious Fundamentalism and Suicide Terrorism

The above represents understandings of nationalist-separatist terrorist psychology. What of religious fundamentalist terrorist psychology? Here we have individuals who are "killing in the name of God." Their acts have been given sacred significance

Photo Removed Due to Copyright Restrictions

In April 2006, Sinn Fein President Gerry Adams speaks at a ceremony marking the 90th anniversary of the beginning of the uprising of the Irish rebels against the British in Northern Ireland.

Photo Removed Due to Copyright Restrictions

One year later, on May 8, 2007, Northern Ireland's First Minister Ian Paisley (left) and Deputy First Minister Martin McGuinness of Sinn Fein were sworn in as power-sharing executive ministers of the Northern Ireland Assembly at the Stormont Parliamentary Building in Belfast.

Nor was joining the group an unusual experience. In fact, when we asked why they joined, we were told that everyone was joining, that anyone who didn't enlist during that period (*intifada*) would have been ostracized.

The cause was passed on early in childhood. There was a generational transmission of hatred between "us" and "them." The children had heard from their parents, whether in the pubs of Northern Ireland or the coffeehouses of Beirut and the occupied territories, what "they" had done to "us," how "they" had stolen our lands, had humiliated "us." Loyal to their parents, who had been damaged by the regime, they were carrying out acts of revenge against "them."

by the radical cleric, be he an ayatollah, rabbi, minister, or priest. And because they are "true believers" who accept uncritically the radical cleric's interpretation of scripture, they do not have the same ambivalence about the extent of violence that the nationalist-separatists do.

One of the questions we posed to the militant Islamist terrorists from Hezbollah and Hamas whom we interviewed concerned their justification for their acts of suicide terrorism, since the Quran specifically proscribes suicide. One respondent became quite angry:

Photo Removed Due to Copyright Restrictions

©AP Images/Muhammed Muheisen

Portraits of Palestinian suicide bombers on a wall above pictures of Israeli victims and destroyed Israeli buses at an exhibit at the Birzeit University on the outskirts of the West Bank town of Ramallah. Some Palestinian children collect photos of the bombers.

A martyrdom operation is the highest level of jihad, and highlights the depth of our faith. The bombers are holy fighters who carry out one of the more important articles of faith.

This is not suicide. Suicide is weak, it is selfish, it is mentally disturbed. This is istishad *[martyrdom or self-sacrifice in the name of Allah.]*

Noted terrorism scholar Ariel Merari made a remarkable observation in the fall of 2004, indicating just how "normal" suicide terrorism was. He indicated that, as he walked around Harvard Square (in Massachusetts), he was struck that teenagers are teenagers the world around. When I asked him what he meant, he told me that:

When I walked into a pizza parlor in Cambridge, the teenagers would be gossiping about their favorite [football] team, the New England Patriots (this was during their run-up to the Super Bowl), about their heroes on the team such as the quarterback, Tom Brady, and how some day, when they grew up, they wanted to be a professional football star like their heroes. Same thing in the refugee camps in the occupied territories; only their favorite team was Hamas, their heroes were the shahids (martyrs), and someday, when they grew up, they wanted to be a shahid like their heroes. It was chillingly normal.

Hassan Salame, a prolific Palestinian suicide bomb commander, has stated:

There is not a mono-causal explanation for the psychology of suicide terrorism. Mohammad Hafez, in his *Manufacturing Human Bombs*,[3] identifies three conditions as prerequisites: a culture of martyrdom, strategic deacons to employ this tactic, and a supply of willing volunteers. In fact, for two of the groups that were most prolific in employing this technique, the Tamil Tigers and the PKK (the Kurdish separatist group), there was no relation to Islamist fundamentalism.

Israeli social scientists developed biographical postmortems of a sample of 93 Palestinian suicide bombers. Seventeen-to-22-year-old young men, they were uneducated, unemployed, unmarried. In fact, they were unformed youth who were told by the suicide bomb commanders when they entered the safe house: "You have a worthless life ahead of you (the unemployment statistics in the camps were 40 to 70 percent, especially for those who had not completed high school), you can do something significant with your life, you will be enrolled in the hall of martyrs, your family will gain prestige, they will be proud of you, and they will get financial benefits." From the time they entered the safe house, they were not alone, with someone sleeping in the same room with them the night before the action to ensure that they did not backslide, and being physically escorted to the site of the "martyrdom operation."

In contrast, the suicide hijackers of September11, 2001, were older (28 to 33 years of age); the ringleader, Mohammad Atta, who was 33, and two of his colleagues were in graduate school in the Technological University in Hamburg. They came from comfortable middle-class

Saudi and Egyptian families. They were fully formed adults who had subordinated their individuality to the destructive charismatic leadership of Osama bin Laden. His cause became the primary mission for his followers. Interestingly, unlike the Palestinian suicide bombers, they had been on their own for upwards of seven years in the West, subjected to the opportunities and temptations of Western democracy, and they simulated blending in while keeping an internal laser-beam focus on their mission to die while taking thousands of innocent casualties.

New Challenges

A particularly alarming development in terms of the social psychology of terrorism, especially intense in Western Europe, is the radicalization of second-generation Muslim immigrants. Their parents had come to Great Britain, France, Germany, the Netherlands, Belgium, and Spain to find a better life, but remained culturally separate, and the second generation became secondarily radicalized, as exemplified by the Madrid train station bombing of March 11, 2004, and the London transit bombings of July 7, 2005.

A particularly daunting challenge is posed by the "new media," both the continuous cable news channels like Al Jazeera, and especially the Internet. Gabriel Weimann estimated in *Terror on the Internet*[4] that in 2006 there were some 4,800 radical Islamist Web sites spinning out their message of anti-Western hatred, contributing to the collective identities of tomorrow's terrorists.

What are the implications for counterterrorism? If one accepts the premise that terrorism is a vicious species of psychological warfare, waged through the media, one doesn't counter it with smart bombs and missiles but with counter-psychological warfare.[5] This suggests four elements of an information operations program:

- Inhibit potential terrorists from joining the group
- Produce dissension in the group
- Facilitate exit from the group
- Reduce support for the group and delegitimate its leaders

But, as noted in one of the conclusions of the Madrid summit working group: "It will require decades to change the culture of hatred and violence. In this struggle, the moral high ground needs to be maintained, for example, by strengthening the rule of law and exemplifying good governance and social justice. To depart from these standards is to lower ourselves to the level of the terrorists and to damage liberal democracy."[6] ∎

The opinions expressed in this article do not necessarily reflect the views or policies of the U.S. government.

Endnotes

1. Jerrold Post, "The Psychological Roots of Terrorism," in *Addressing the Causes of Terrorism: The Club de Madrid Series on Democracy and Terrorism*, vol. 1 (Madrid: Club de Madrid, 2005).

2. Jerrold Post, E. Sprinzak, and L. Denny, "The Terrorists in Their Own Words: Interviews With 35 Incarcerated Middle Eastern Terrorists," *Terrorism and Political Violence*, vol. 15, no. 1 (2003): pp. 171-184.

3. Mohammed Hafez, *Manufacturing Human Bombs: The Making of Palestinian Suicide Bombers* (Washington, D.C.: United States Institute of Peace, 2006).

4. Gabriel Weimann, *Terror on the Internet: The New Arena, the New Challenges* (Washington, D.C.: United States Institute of Peace, 2006).

5. For an expansion of the manner in which psychological operations should play a central role in countering terrorism, see Jerrold Post, "Psychological Operations and Counter-terrorism," *Joint Force Quarterly*, issue 37 (Spring 2005): pp. 105-110.

6. Jerrold Post, "The Psychological Roots of Terrorism," in *Addressing the Causes of Terrorism: The Club de Madrid Series on Democracy and Terrorism*, vol. 1 (Madrid: Club de Madrid, 2005), p. 11.

Women as Victims and Victimizers

Mia Bloom

Mia Bloom, PhD, is an assistant professor in the School of Public and International Affairs at the University of Georgia in Athens, Georgia.

Photo Removed Due to Copyright Restrictions

This Iraqi woman, whose son is missing following a suicide car bomb attack at a police checkpoint in Baghdad, Iraq, in September 2005, is only one of the thousands of victims of terrorism.

On November 9, 2005, Muriel Degauque, a Belgian convert to radical Islam, blew herself up in a suicide car bombing in Iraq. That same day, Sajida Atrous al-Rishawi's explosive belt failed to detonate at a hotel wedding reception in Amman.

Despite the shock associated with the above events, women have long been involved in terrorist movements. In the 1970s and 1980s, many were prominently active in Latin American and European terrorist organizations and, depending on the group, may have constituted as much as one-third of the personnel—as was the case of Germany's Red Army Faction and Second of June Movement. However, the migration of women functioning from mostly supportive roles to more active, operational roles, such as suicide bombers, is much more recent. The first was a 17-year-old Lebanese girl who blew herself up near an Israeli convoy in 1985. This growing role of women in terrorism has caused new questions to surface.

Out of the approximately 17 groups that have used the tactic of suicide bombing, women have been operatives in more than half. Between 1985 and 2006, there were more than 220 women suicide bombers, representing about 15 percent of the total number of such attacks. Moreover, the upsurge in the number of female bombers has come from both secular and religious organizations, even though religious groups initially resisted the use of women in such contexts.[1]

Since September 2005, when a female suicide bomber set off a blast in the northwest city of Tal Afar that killed eight Iraqi army recruits and wounded 30, several more such cases have emerged in Iraq. That December, two women blew themselves up in a classroom at Baghdad's police academy, killing 27, and as recently as February 25, 2007, a female bomber killed 42 and injured 51 at Baghdad's second largest college, Mustansiriyah University.

The Question of "Why"

It is typical following such events for the media to dissect the presumed motivations of the bomber, but the overwhelming reaction is shock that a woman—usually perceived as the victim, not the perpetrator, of violence—would do such a thing. Terrorism experts, psychologists, and political analysts frequently engage in developing a "psychological autopsy," examining where the perpetrator grew up, where she went to school, and what went wrong to make her turn to violence. A common assumption is that she must be depressed, crazy, suicidal, or psychopathic, and, overwhelmingly, that it must have been a man who made her do it.

However, years of research finds psychopathology and personality disorder no more likely among terrorists than among non-terrorists from the same communities. And although we no longer believe men force most women into terrorism, the men in these women's lives play an important role in mobilizing them to terrorism. According to Deborah Galvin, "Some women are recruited into terrorist organizations by boyfriends. A significant feature

Photo Removed Due to Copyright Restrictions

In February 2006, female Iranian students fill out registration forms indicating their readiness to carry out suicide attacks.

that may characterize the involvement of the female terrorist is the male or female lover/female accomplice ... scenario."[2] In fact, though al-Rishawi failed in her attempt to kill the Amman wedding celebrants, her husband, who accompanied her, succeeded in murdering 38.

The British journalist Eileen MacDonald relates how "Begona" explained joining the ETA (the Basque nationalist terrorist group in Spain and France) at age 25 "because a man I knew was a member."[3] Rumors also abound of men seducing women into participation in violence through sexual misconduct, requiring a subsequent "act of martyrdom" as the only way to purify the family name and save face. Nevertheless, it is misleading to assume that women are merely victims or pawns of men without any political motivation of their own. In fact, one of the most reliable predictors of a women's involvement in a particular movement is her relationship to a former or current terrorist in that movement. In al-Rishawi's case, several of her brothers had been killed in Iraq fighting in the insurgency against Coalition troops, while her marriage of a few days had been arranged to facilitate the operation.

Some psychologists explain that terrorists typically suffer from "narcissistic injuries"—essentially, a lasting damage to their self-image and self-esteem severe enough to force the discredited self to seek a new, "positive identity" (i.e., achieving a sense of "belonging" as a member of a terrorist group). Psychologist Joseph Margolin argues that "much terrorist behavior is a response to the frustration of various political, economic, and personal needs or objectives."[4] Dr. Randy Borum adds:

"The link between frustration (being prevented from attaining a goal or engaging in a behavior) and aggression [may be] a 'master explanation' for understanding the cause of human violence."[5] Other experts go so far as to assert that most terrorists are borderline autistic, and thus gravitate to the ideologies that simplify the world into black and white, good and evil.[6]

Root Causes

Authors from the fields of psychology, sociology, and political science all identify root causes as key to understanding why most terrorism occurs. Much of what is listed as a root cause, however, also explains mobilization of non-terrorist political groups and, therefore, falls into the category of "necessary though insufficient" explanations for why these factors result, for some, in a turn to violence. They include:
- Lack of democracy, civil liberties, and the rule of law
- Failed or weak states that provide havens for terrorists
- Too rapid modernization
- Extremist ideologies—both secular and religious
- A history of political violence, civil wars, revolutions, dictatorships, or occupation
- Illegitimate or corrupt governments
- Repression by foreign occupation or colonial powers
- The experience of discrimination on the basis of ascriptive (ethnic, racial, or religious) characteristics
- Social injustice
- The presence of charismatic ideological leaders[7]

According to experts like Yoram Schweitzer and Farhana Ali, women tend to be motivated by reasons that are more "personal" than those that influence men. These can be summarized as the four R's: Revenge, Redemption, Respect, and Relationship. In particular, they include:
- The loss of a loved one (usually the dominant male in their life—their husband, father, or brother)
- A need to reinvent themselves because of alleged or real sexual misconduct
- An inability to conceive children or being considered not marriageable[8]
- A desire to improve the status of women in their society
- Proof that they are just as dedicated as the men to the Cause
- Being the sisters, daughters, or wives of well-known insurgents[9]

Photo Removed Due to Copyright Restrictions

During a 2004 rally in support of Hamas, a Palestinian boy holds a photograph of a woman who blew herself up at the major crossing point between Israel and the Gaza Strip, killing four Israelis.

Differences and Similarities

Assuming, however, that women are motivated by reasons different from those influencing men is problematic. Like men, most women are inspired by both personal and political reasons to engage in violence. Psychologist Ariel Merari states: "Culture in general and religion in particular seem to be relatively unimportant in the phenomenon of terrorist suicide. Terrorist suicide, like any other suicide, is basically an individual rather than a group phenomenon: People who wish to die for personal reasons do it. The terrorist framework simply offers the excuse (rather than the real drive) for doing it and the legitimacy for carrying it out in a violent way."[10]

For both male and female terrorists, the cause includes a view of the world that makes sense of their imminent death and often links them to some form of "immortality." Recently, there is a tendency to assume a natural connection between faith and the willingness to kill and

be killed.[11] However, no *a-priori* link between religion and terror has thus far been established.

In fact, historically, many terrorist groups—such as the Red Brigades in Italy, the Red Army Faction in Germany, and the Shining Path in Peru—were radical-socialists with no religious connection whatsoever. They did, however, include the liberation of women as part of their political program.

Most women involved in terrorism today appear to fulfill a role as inexpensive cannon fodder. In general, it appears they have become a tactical innovation because they deviate from established counterterrorist profiles and stereotypes. Furthermore, as anyone who has watched the movie *The Battle of Algiers* can attest, female operatives can easily blend in with the enemy's civilian population for reconnaissance purposes: Their clothing readily hides bombs, and they sometimes use the appearance of being pregnant to discourage searches. But, in fact, few women are permitted to engage in leadership functions, even in groups where they comprise 30 to 60 percent of the bombers. According to Clara Beyler, speaking of the use of Palestinian terrorist organizations: "Women are rarely involved in the higher echelons of the decision-making process of these groups. Women may volunteer, or ... women might be coerced to conduct a murderous strike, but the woman's role is ultimately dictated by the patriarchal hierarchy that rules Palestinian society and its terrorist groups."[12]

In reality, those who engage in violence are few relative to any overall movement. Since terrorists are but a fraction of the group they purport to represent, their real opposition is often from moderates in their own community who prefer alternatives to violence. Terrorists, therefore, seek to force a violent counter-response from authorities that will elicit sympathy and support, radicalize more members of the community, and help mobilize more recruits. By using female operatives, terrorist organizations hope for overreaction against the women of their society, a surefire way to elicit further outrage and anger.

No General Patterns

A principal goal of terrorism is to foster fear and uncertainty beyond the immediate victims by destroying lives and property in hopes of causing greater long-term costs. Terrorists want the enemy to expend time and money bolstering security; their desire is to charge an enormous tax on the enemy's society, forcing it to transfer resources from production to anti-productive measures.[13]

One potentially useful counterterrorism initiative is to appeal to the larger community and bolster moderates. Addressing the root causes may not eliminate violence, but it might help to show that moderates are able to deliver benefits to the population while the terrorists cannot. Most surveys indicate that the support for violence decreases when there are viable alternatives and better prospects for peace.[14]

For women, it is important to emphasize that they can play a positive role in their societies and make a greater and more meaningful contribution in life than in death. It would help to support women's grassroots organizations that benefit the community as a whole. Such groups can form the backbone of a civil society that can bridge different communities and lay the groundwork for the emergence of real democracy.[15]

The most important issues to make clear are that there are no general patterns, no reliable profiles, and no way to explain every kind of terrorism.

Psychologist John Horgan explains that every terrorist movement is complex in its own way, and that even the smallest of groups are characterized by a variety of roles leading to "different kinds of involvement"[16] both for men and women. Furthermore, there are so many different kinds of terrorism, conducted for different reasons, that it is not possible to identify a single cause of any individual form of terrorism—Islamist, global Salafist, single issue (e.g., environmental, animal rights), right-wing racist, nationalist-separatist—let alone one that explains the motivations for all women.

I have argued elsewhere that there are calculated organizational motivations for using women. The leaders of terrorist movements make cost-benefit calculations to select tactics, targets, and perpetrators, and women suicide bombers are cheap weapons. Further, they garner significantly more media attention and may also shame men into becoming mobilized instead of letting women "do their job."[17]

Undeniably, however, more useful data could be obtained if researchers could speak directly with members of known foreign terrorist movements. Although access to such primary sources has been limited,[18] as Horgan argues: "Unpalatable as it may seem, it is inevitable that to understand the development and structure of terrorist behavior, we have to meet with and speak to people who have been, or are, involved in terrorist violence."[19] This is particularly true in determining why women, traditionally nurturers, choose to become killers. ∎

The opinions expressed in this article do not necessarily reflect the views or policies of the U.S. government.

Endnotes

1. Mia Bloom, "Female Suicide Bombers: A Global Trend," *Deadalus* (Winter 2007).

2. Deborah M. Galvin, "The Female Terrorist: A Socio-Psychological Perspective," *Behavioral Science and the Law*, vol. 1 (1983): pp.19–32.

3. Eileen MacDonald, *Shoot the Women First* (New York: Random House, 1992).

4. Joseph Margolin, "Psychological Perspectives in Terrorism," in Y. Alexander and S. M. Finger (eds.), *Terrorism: Interdisciplinary Perspectives* (New York: John Jay, 1977), pp. 273-274.

5. Randy Borum, *Psychology of Terrorism* (Tampa, FL: University of Florida, 2004), p. 13.

6. D. Gambetta and S. Hertog, "Engineers of Jihad," unpublished paper presented to the Centre for the Study of Civil War (17 August 2006).

7. T. Björgo, *Root Causes of Terrorism* (London: Routledge, 2005).

8. R. Pape, *Dying to Win: The Strategic Logic of Suicide Terror* (New York: Random House, 2005).

9. Noor Huda Ismail, "Married to a Jihadist," *Straits Times* (10 March 2006). Available at http://noorhudaismail.blogspot.com/2006/03/married-to-jihadist.html.

10. Ariel Merari, "The Readiness to Kill and Die: Suicidal Terrorism in the Middle East," in W. Reich (ed.), *Origins of Terrorism: Psychologies, Ideologies, Theologies and States of Mind* (New York: Cambridge University Press, 1990), p. 206.

11. See for example M. Jurgensmeyer, *Terror in the Mind of God: The Global Rise of Religious Violence* (Berkeley, CA: University of California Press, 2003); J. Stern, *Terror in the Name of God: Why Religious Militants Kill* (New York: Random House, 2004); and J. Esposito, *Unholy War: Terror in the Name of Islam* (London: Oxford University Press, 2002).

12. Clara Beyler, "Using Palestinian Women as Bombs," *New York Sun* (15 November 2006).

13. C. McCauley, "The Psychology of Terrorism." Available at *http://www.ssrc.org/sept11/essays/mccauley.htm.*

14. Mia Bloom, *Dying to Kill: The Allure of Suicide Terror* (New York: Columbia University Press, 2005), ch. 3 passim.

15. A. Varshney, *Ethnic Conflict and Civic Life: Hindus and Muslims in India* (New Haven, CT: Yale University Press, 2003).

16. John Horgan, *The Psychology of Terrorism.* (London: Routledge, 2005).

17. Bloom, M., *Dying to Kill: The Allure of Suicide Terror* (New York: Columbia University Press, 2005).

18. A notable exception is Jerrold Post, E. Sprinzak, and L. Denny, "The Terrorists in Their Own Words: Interviews With 35 Incarcerated Middle Eastern Terrorists," *Terrorism and Political Violence*, vol. 15, no. 1 (2003): pp. 171-184.

19. John Horgan, *The Psychology of Terrorism.* (London: Routledge, 2005) and (2008, forthcoming).

Terrorism: A Brief History

Walter Laqueur

Walter Laqueur, PhD, now retired from his many academic postings, is most recently associated with the International Research Council at the Center for Strategic and International Studies, Washington, D.C., as its former director and, currently, a distinguished scholar.

What is terrorism? There are more than a hundred definitions. The Department of State has one, Title 22 of the U.S. Code Section 2656: "premeditated, politically motivated violence perpetrated against noncombatant targets by subnational groups or clandestine agents, usually intended to influence an audience." The Department of Defense has another, and also the Federal Bureau of Investigation, while the present writer has contributed two or three definitions of his own. But none is wholly satisfactory.

Too much has been made, in my opinion, of the element of "noncombatant targets" in order to define terrorism; there has not been a terrorist group in history that has attacked only soldiers or policemen. And what if a group of gunmen attack soldiers in the morning and civilians at night: Are they terrorists, do they belong to a different category, or do they change their character in the course of a day?

No all-embracing definition will ever be found for the simple reason that there is not one terrorism, but there have been many terrorisms, greatly differing in time and space, in motivation, and in manifestations and aims.

Initial Studies

When the systematic study of terrorism began in the 1970s, it was—mistakenly—believed by some that terrorism was more or less a monopoly of extreme left-wing groups, such as the Italian Red Brigades or the German Red Army or various Latin American groups. (There was also ethnic-nationalist terrorism, such as in Northern Ireland, but it figured less prominently.) Hence the conclusion: Terrorism comes into being wherever people are most exploited and most cruelly oppressed. Terrorism, therefore, could easily be ended by removing exploitation and oppression.

However, it should have been clear even then that this could not possibly be a correct explanation because terrorism had been altogether absent precisely in the most oppressive regimes of the 20th century—Nazi Germany and Stalinist Russia. True, there was virtually no terrorism in the very richest societies and the most egalitarian—but nor was there terrorism in the very poorest.

A decade passed and most of the terrorist groups of the Far Left disappeared. If there was terrorism during the 1980s, it came to large extent from small cells of the Extreme Right. There were some instances of aircraft hijackings and bombings (such as over Lockerbie, Scotland), and a few embassies were attacked or even seized (such as in Tehran), but these operations were not carried out by groups of the Extreme Left.

Photo Removed Due to Copyright Restrictions

Investigators examine the remains of Pan Am flight 103, which exploded over Lockerbie, Scotland, on December 22, 1988. All 259 persons on board and 11 people on the ground died. The victims and debris were strewn over an area of 2,189 square kilometers.

The most deadly terrorist act in the United States prior to September 11, 2001, was the 1995 bombing of a federal building in Oklahoma City, carried out by right-wing extremist sectarians. Nationalist terrorism continued (in Ulster, the Basque region of Spain, Sri Lanka, Israel, and some other places), but the Islamist terrorism that figures so prominently today was, as yet, hardly in appearance except, sporadically, in some Middle Eastern countries.

Today, terrorism and al-Qaida, and similar groups motivated by religious fanaticism, have virtually become synonyms, inevitably, perhaps, because most contemporary terrorism is carried out by their adherents. But the temptation to equate terrorism with these groups should be resisted for the simple reason that terrorism antedates militant Islamism by a very long time and, for all one knows, will continue to exist well after the present protagonists of jihadism have disappeared.

Terrorism is not a political doctrine, even though some have attempted to transform it into an ideology; it is, instead, one of the oldest forms of violence—even though it goes without saying that not all violence is terrorism. It probably antedates regular warfare because the fighting of armies involves a certain amount of organization and sophisticated logistics that primitive man did not have.

Historical Background

Terrorism appears in the Bible's Old Testament, and there were frequent incidents of political murder, even systematic assassination, in Greek and Roman history. The murder of Julius Caesar, to give but one example, preoccupied writers and artists for the next two millennia. The question of whether tyrannicide (such as undertaken by William Tell, the national hero of Swiss sagas) was permissible kept generations of theologians and philosophers busy.

There was no total unanimity, but the majority opinion was that terrorism was permissible in certain conditions. When a cruel oppressor—a tyrant—being an enemy of all mankind, in violation of the law of God and human justice, left his victims no other way out of intolerable oppression, commission of a terrorist act was *ultima ratio*, the last refuge of the oppressed, all other means having been exhausted.

But philosophers and theologians were aware even then that there was a grave danger of misusing the doctrine of justifiable tyrannicide, claiming *ultima ratio* when, in fact, there was no justifiable reason for killing (such as

Photo Removed Due to Copyright Restrictions

The assassination of Archduke Franz Ferdinand of Austria and his wife by a Pan-Slavism nationalist group during the royals' visit to Sarajevo, Bosnia, on June 28, 1914, precipitated World War I.

in the case of the murder of the good King Henri IV of France) or when there existed other ways to express protest and resistance.

In the meantime, small groups engaging in systematic terrorism over long periods had arisen, such as the secret sect of the Assassins, an offshoot of the Muslim Ismailis, which operated from the 8th into the 14th century from what is now Iraq and Iran, killing governors, prefects, caliphs, and a crusader king of Jerusalem. They pioneered suicide terrorism—their weapon was always the dagger, and since their victims were usually well guarded, the chances of escaping were virtually nil. Even the language they used has survived—a fighter was a *fida'i*, a term used to this day.

Terrorism continued to be active through the end of the Middle Ages into Modern Times, though on a somewhat reduced scale. This was the age of great wars such as the Thirty Years War (1618-1648) and the Napoleonic Wars (1799-1815). And in such periods, when a great many people were killed and wounded on the battlefields, no one would pay much attention if terrorist violence occurred here and there on a small scale.

The High Tide of Terrorism

The high tide of terrorism rose toward the end of the 19th century. Among the main active groups were the Irish rebels, the Russian Socialist Revolutionaries, and assorted anarchists all over Europe and North America. But secret societies were also actively engaging in terrorism outside Europe—in Egypt, for instance, as well as in India and China—aiming at national liberation. Some of these attacks had tragic consequences; others were more successful in the long, rather than the short, run.

The violence of the 19th century terrorists was notable—they killed a Russian tsar (Alexander II), as well as many ministers, archdukes, and generals; American presidents (William McKinley in 1901 and, before him in 1881, James Garfield); King Umberto of Italy; an empress of the Austro-Hungarian monarchy; Sadi Carnot, president of France; Antonio Canovas, the Spanish prime minister—to mention only some of the most prominent victims. The First World War, of course, was triggered by the murder of Franz Ferdinand, the Austrian heir to the throne, in Sarajevo in 1914.

Rereading the press of that period (and also novels by leading writers from Fyodor Dostoevsky to Henry James and Joseph Conrad), one could easily gain the impression that terrorism was the greatest danger facing mankind and that the end of civilized life was at hand. But as so often before and after, the terrorist danger passed, and, as the Russian Bolshevik revolutionary Leon Trotsky noted on one occasion, one minister was killed, but several others were only too eager to replace him.

Photo Removed Due to Copyright Restrictions

Three unidentified people wearing Basque berets and seated in front of an ETA flag appeared on a 2006 television video. ETA (Euskadi Ta Askatasuna, or Basque Homeland and Freedom), which seeks a Basque state independent from Spain, is a designated terrorist group.

Contemporary Terrorism

Terrorism reappeared after World War I in various countries, such as Germany and the Balkan nations. Before coming to power, both Fascists and Communists believed in mass violence rather than individual terrorist acts—with some occasional exceptions, such as the assassination of the Italian Socialist leader Giacomo Matteoti.

There was little terrorism during World War II and during the two decades thereafter. This explains, perhaps, why the renewal of terrorist operations in the 1970s and, *a fortiori*, the appearance of Islamist terrorism were interpreted by many, oblivious of the long, earlier history of terrorism, as something wholly new and unprecedented. This was particularly striking with regard to suicide terrorism. As noted earlier, most terrorism up to the late 19th century had been suicide missions, simply because

the only available weapons were daggers, short-range pistols, or highly unstable bombs likely to explode in the hands of the attackers.

It is true, however, that contemporary terrorism differs in some essential respects from that perpetrated in the 19th century and earlier on.

Traditional terrorism had its "code of honor": It targeted kings, military leaders, ministers, and other leading public figures, but if there were a danger that the wife or the children of the target would be killed in an attack, terrorists would refrain from striking, even if doing so endangered their own lives.

Today, indiscriminate terrorism has become the rule; very few leading politicians or generals have been killed, but very many wholly innocent people have. The term terrorism has, therefore, very negative connotations, and terrorists now insist on being called by another name. When Boris Savinkov, who headed the Russian Socialist Revolutionaries before World War I, published his autobiography, he had no hesitation in giving it the title *Memoirs of a Terrorist*. Today this would be unthinkable—the modern terrorist wants to be known as a freedom fighter, a guerrilla, a militant, an insurgent, a rebel, a revolutionary—anything but a terrorist, a killer of random innocents.

If there is no agreement concerning a definition of terrorism, does it mean that total confusion and relativism prevail, that one view is as good as another? It is perfectly true that, as an often quoted saying goes, one person's terrorist is another's freedom fighter. But since even the greatest mass murderers in history had their admirers, from Hitler to Pol Pot, such wisdom does not take us very far. Most of those who have studied terrorism and are reasonably free from bias will agree much of the time in their judgment of an action, even if perfect definitions of terrorism do not exist. Someone has compared it with pornography or obscenity, which is also difficult to define, but an observer with some experience will know it when he sees it.

There are no shortcuts to explain why people choose to be terrorists, no magic formulas or laws similar to Newton's and Einstein's in the physical world. From time to time, new insights are offered that do not, however, usually survive critical examination. Recently, for instance, it has been suggested that terrorism occurs only (or mainly) where there has been a foreign invasion of a country. This proposition is true in some cases, such as Napoleon's occupation of Spain or the presence of U.S. troops in Iraq. But a look at the geopolitical map of contemporary terrorism shows that, in most cases, from Sri Lanka to Bangladesh to Algeria to Europe, foreign invasion is not the decisive factor. And even in Iraq, the great majority of terrorist victims occur not among the occupying forces but as the result of attacks of Sunnis against Shiites, and vice versa.

A Generational Phenomenon

Does history offer any lessons?

Again, there are no clear-cut answers except in a very general way. Terrorism has seldom, if ever, occurred in effective dictatorships. In the modern world, it appears, ironically, that terrorists take advantage of the freedoms of thought, speech, religion, movement, and assembly offered by democracies. Terrorism is also a problem of failed states in which central power is weak or nonexistent. There was, for example, virtually no terrorism from the street in Franco's Spain, but as his dictatorship was dismantled, it appeared on the political scene. In the Middle East, even

Photo Removed Due to Copyright Restrictions

Former hostage Victor Amburgy hugs an unidentified child after his arrival back in the United States on July 2, 1985. Amburgy was among the 153 international passengers and crew of TWA flight 847, hijacked by Lebanese terrorists shortly after its June 14 takeoff from Greece and held for two weeks.

mildly authoritarian regimes have put down terrorism without great difficulty—Turkey and Syria in the 1980s, Algeria and Egypt in the decade thereafter.

Terrorism has sometimes succeeded but, at least equally and probably more often, has failed to attain its aims. And in some cases, it has resulted in the opposite of what its perpetrators wanted to achieve.

But terrorism is largely a generational phenomenon, and even if defeated, it may recur at a later date. There is no good reason to expect the disappearance of terrorism in our time. In an age in which large-scale wars have become too dangerous and expensive, terrorism is the prevailing form of violent conflict. As long as there are conflicts on Earth, there will be terrorism. ■

The opinions expressed in this article do not necessarily reflect the views or policies of the U.S. government.

From Profiles to Pathways: The Road to Recruitment

John Horgan

Photo Removed Due to Copyright Restrictions

Iranian men register their readiness to be suicide "martyrs" at an April 2006 recruitment rally in Tehran.

John Horgan, PhD, is senior research fellow at the Centre for the Study of Terrorism and Political Violence, and lecturer in international relations at the University of St. Andrews, Scotland. An Irish political psychologist, his Dr. Horgan's most recent research is focused on movement into and out of terrorist groups. His book, Walking Away from Terrorism: Accounts of Disengagement from Radical and Extremist Movements, *will be published in 2008.*

Less than a year after four coordinated suicide bombings targeted London's underground rail system on July 7, 2005, an eagerly awaited House of Commons Report[1] into the events of that day concluded: "What we know of previous extremists in the UK shows that there is not a consistent profile to help identify who may be vulnerable to radicalization. Of the four individuals here, three were second-generation British citizens whose parents were of Pakistani origin and one whose parents were of Jamaican origin; Kamel Bourgass, convicted of the Ricin plot, was an Algeria failed asylum seeker; Richard Reid, the failed shoe bomber, had an English mother and Jamaican father. ... Some have been well-educated, some less so. Some genuinely poor, some less so. Some apparently well integrated in the UK, others not. Most single, but some family men with children. Some previously law-abiding, others with a history of petty crime."

Implicit throughout this remarkable report was a sense of frustration at the failure to arrive at a clear profile of those who have been recruited into al-Qaida's global campaign of terrorism and subversion. That same frustration is, in fact, apparent in many policy and law enforcement circles, and despite the failure by researchers to arrive at any valid and reliable terrorist profile, the search for one continues.

Profiling the Terrorist

However, notwithstanding the evidence that, logically, terrorist profiles are unlikely to emerge at all,[2] that this search continues unabated is hardly surprising. There are some clear and understandable issues that drive the attempts to profile.

On the one hand, the dramatic consequences of successful terrorist activity force us to confront the effects of behavior that would, to most normal people, suggest abnormality or some sort of sickness—"how could anyone do this?" being a typical response to the shocking behavior associated with terrorist attacks.

A second issue that drives profiling efforts is another basic question: Given that so *many* people are exposed to the presumed generating conditions for terrorism (or "root causes"), the triggering factors and catalysts—both for religious and political mobilization—that may lead to engagement in violent activity, why is it that so *few* people actually become recruited?

This is a difficult question to answer, and any answer we do provide will certainly not be satisfactory to all. A temptation, which has heavily influenced the nature and direction of some prior research (especially from psychologists), has been to assume that some qualities of specialness exist both within a specific group of terrorists—in terms of what makes them "alike"—as well as what presumably makes them "different" from the rest of us (or at least to those who do not engage in terrorism).

Psychologist and terrorism expert Ariel Merari has correctly argued that it is more precise to state that "no terrorist profile has been found" rather than that "there is no terrorist profile."[3] However, I would strongly argue that there are several real dangers associated with the continued effort to construct such profiles, particularly as far as understanding recruitment to terrorism is concerned.

In assuming the existence of a profile, we tend to miss several critical features associated with the development of the terrorist. These include, but are not limited to:

- The gradual nature of the relevant socialization processes into terrorism
- A sense of the supportive qualities associated with that reruitment (e.g., the "pull" factors, or lures, that attract people to either involvement in terrorism in a broad sense, or those positive lures that are used to groom potential recruits)
- The sense of migration between roles (e.g., moving from fringe activity such as public protest to illegal, focused behavior—in other words, moving from one role to another)
- A sense of the importance of role qualities (e.g., what attractions does being a sniper hold as opposed to becoming a suicide bomber, and how do these "role qualities" become apparent to the onlooker or potential recruit?)

When we assume static qualities of the terrorist (a feature of profiles), we become blind to the factors and dynamics that shape and support the development of the terrorist. One further consequence is that we also obscure the basis from which a more practical counterterrorism strategy might develop to prevent or control the extent of those who initially become involved in terrorism.

Those who work in counterterrorism, however, frequently rely on profiles. Having recently delivered a presentation on terrorist profiling before an audience of counterterrorism officials, a senior official protested to me, "Profiles are useful. Of course they are. The reason … is that your average suicide bomber is not going to be the middle-aged, white, father of three kids." This comment was made in the United Kingdom, where, obviously, this response can be understood by virtue of the fact that we have not seen a suicide bomber of this kind there *yet*.

The point here is not to feed into an anything-is-possible exaggeration and distortion of the threat, but to be mindful that the assumptions that feed into how we think about the terrorist are based increasingly on the actuarial projections from a small, and statistically insignificant, sample of individuals. The dangers of overgeneralization should be obvious.

But highlighting these limitations still does not answer the critical question: Why does one person become involved in terrorism and the other not? Without a doubt, it is practically impossible to answer this question satisfactorily, but we do have some helpful starting points. In a recent book,[4] I have identified a series of what I have termed predisposing risk factors for involvement in terrorism. In no particular order, these include:

- Personal experiences of victimization (which can be real or imagined)
- Expectations about involvement (e.g., the lures—such as excitement, mission, sense of purpose—associated with being involved in any "insider" group and its various roles)
- Identification with a cause, frequently associated with some victimized community
- Socialization through friends or family, or being raised in a particular environment
- Opportunity for expression of interest and steps toward involvement
- Access to the relevant group

It must be stated that, individually, none of these will ever help explain why people become terrorists, but, taken in combination, they do provide a powerful framework for understanding why one person might become involved in terrorism and another does not.

Terrorist Pathways

In order to move beyond rather sterile and unhelpful debates about profiling, it might be useful to consider what involvement in terrorism implies so that we begin to move toward what I would argue are more fruitful avenues for psychologically informed counterterrorism initiatives.

Foremost among these is that the reality of involvement in terrorism today is typified by its *complexity*. Involvement in terrorism seems to imply—and result in—very different things to very different people.[5] This also seems to be the case within the same group, as well as across the spectrum of terrorist movements. Far from the simplistic distinctions between leaders and followers, even the smallest of terrorist movements comprise a variety of roles and functions into which recruits are assigned or encouraged to move toward, depending on a plethora of factors. Additionally, adoption and retention of those roles is neither discrete nor static. There is very often migration both between and within roles, from illegal (e.g., engaging in violent activity) to grey areas (supporting the engagement in violent activity) to legal (e.g., peaceful protest).

While many of the activities that terrorist movements engage in are not actually illegal per se (and cannot be meaningfully encompassed under the label "terrorism," but perhaps instead "subversion"), without them actual terrorist operations could not exist.

For the most part, engagement in violent activity is that which we most commonly associate with terrorism. However, the reality of terrorist movements today is that this most public of roles and functions tends to merely represent the tip of an iceberg of activity. Supporting the execution of a violent attack are those directly aiding and abetting the event, those who house the terrorist or provide other kinds of support, those who raise funds, generate publicity, provide intelligence, and so forth.

The person we think of as "the terrorist" is therefore fulfilling only one, albeit the most dramatic in terms of direct consequences, of multiple functions in the movement.

One consequence of the complexity of these issues is the obvious need for the development of more imaginative and flexible counterterrorism initiatives. If we were to stretch the continuum of functions associated with terrorist movements outward even more, we would see that the farther away we move from the violence associated with terrorism, the more we move toward identifying functions

Photo Removed Due to Copyright Restrictions

Being raised in an environment in which terrorism is glorified and associated with excitement is a risk factor for involvement in terrorism activity.

that become increasingly difficult to classify either as terrorism or even illegal. Put another way, there is much more to terrorist movements than "terrorism."

Avenues for Counterterrorism

How people move between and within roles (i.e, migration and promotion, respectively) is poorly understood. Overall, we can say that involvement in terrorism is a complex process, comprising discrete phases that could be encapsulated as an individual terrorist engages in a gradual process of accommodation and assimilation across incrementally experienced stages.

There is a sense of ongoing movement into, through, and, sometimes, out of different roles and functions. Despite the fact that timing will always depend on a host of factors, and some individuals appear to become involved more quickly than others, a constant quality across all terrorist movements is this gradual sense of progression.

The notion of there being a moment of epiphany that explains some assumedly conscious decision to become a terrorist is naïve, misleading, and, crucially, unsupported by empirical evidence.

Furthermore, this process of movement is based on initially supportive qualities: While terrorism will always be a product of its own time and place, and multiple motivations will co-exist for members of even the same movement, the most obvious common denominator influencing individuals' embracement of their own radicalization—at any level—is a sense of positive expectation.

We do not engage in behavior unless we view it as having some distinct benefit to us. The same applies to the behavior of the terrorist. Sometimes that might be expressed in terms of expectations about achieving a sense of status, authority, acceptance, mission, and so forth. And as long as commitment and dedication to one's socialization further and further into the movement remains positive for the follower, this eventually results in the formation of a new—or at least effectively consolidated—identity.

If we want to appreciate what, if anything, is the "terrorist mind," it is probably best thought of as the product of:

- Increased socialization into a terrorist movement and its associated engagement in illegal activity
- Focused behavior, more generally, that is increasingly relevant to the context of a terrorist movement

From a personal and social perspective, this often means that a socialization *into* terrorism, and those associated with it, sees a socialization *away from* nonrelevant friends, family, and the person's former life.

One of several consequences that would seem to emerge from making distinctions between these phases is that we might begin to develop phase-specific counterterrorism initiatives, depending on what it is we can ascertain is the most effective intervention point; that is, whether it be initial prevention of involvement, subsequent disruption of engagement, or eventual facilitation of disengagement. Acknowledging these distinctions will lead us into realizing that there are probably unique kinds of interventions to be developed, depending on where we eventually decide our interventions are best focused.

Despite the fact that the disengagement phase remains the most poorly understood and least researched, ironically, it is in this phase that I would argue that practical counterterrorism initiatives—aimed not only at facilitation of disengagement but at prevention of initial involvement—might actually become more effective.

The Importance of the Individual

While terrorism ultimately is a group activity, that group will always comprise individuals each of whom has a role to play, as outlined above. Although counterterrorism programs generally do not tend to focus on individuals, it is precisely by understanding individual radicalization and its associated social and psychological qualities that we can get a sense of what kinds of dynamics need to be understood in order to develop ways of promoting disengagement.[6]

Although terrorism can bring about significant and large-scale consequences, it remains, in essence, low-level, low-volume, and disproportionate activity perpetrated by individuals. The large-scale significance and impact of terrorism should never deter us from engaging in microanalyses both of the terrorist and of terrorist events. ∎

The opinions expressed in this article do not necessarily reflect the views or policies of the U.S. government.

Endnotes

1. *House of Commons Report of the Official Account of the Bombings in London on 7th July 2005* (London: The Stationery Office, 2006), p. 31.

2. For a detailed explanation, see John Horgan, *The Psychology of Terrorism* (New York: Routledge, 2005).

3. Personal correspondence.

4. John Horgan, *The Psychology of Terrorism* (New York: Routledge, 2005).

5. This issue and its implications are discussed in detail in M. Taylor and J. Horgan, "A Conceptual Framework for Understanding the Development of Psychological Process in the Terrorist," *Terrorism and Political Violence*, vol. 18 (2006): pp. 1-17.

6. Work on this issue has begun at the University of St. Andrews and will be published in 2008. See John Horgan, *Walking Away From Terrorism: Accounts of Disengagement From Radical and Extremist Movements* (New York: Routledge, in press).

Mass-Media Theater

Gabriel Weimann

Gabriel Weimann, PhD, is a professor of communications at Haifa University, Israel, and the School of International Studies at The American University, Washington, D.C. His paper is based on his forthcoming study, The Psychology of Mass-Mediated Terrorism, *supported by the U.S. Institute of Peace, where he has been a research fellow.*

Photo Removed Due to Copyright Restrictions

When one says "terrorism" in a democratic society, one also says "media." For terrorism by its very nature is a psychological weapon which depends upon communicating a threat to a wider society. This, in essence, is why terrorism and the media enjoy a symbiotic relationship.

—Paul Wilkinson[1]

Al-Qaida broadcasts over its own media outlet, the Voice of the Caliphate.

The Psychology of Terror

From its early days, terror has entailed a mass psychological aspect: The word "terror" comes from the Latin word "*terrere*," which means "to frighten or scare." During the 1793 French Revolution, the Reign of Terror resulted in the execution of 17,000 people, all conducted before large audiences and accompanied by sensational publicity, thus spreading the intended fear among any citizens with the temerity to object.

Modern terrorism can be understood in terms of the same production requirements as any theatrical engagement: meticulous attention paid to script preparation, cast selection, sets, props, role-playing, and minute-by-minute stage management. And just like compelling stage plays or ballet performances, the media orientation of terrorist activity requires careful attention to detail in order to be effective. The victim is, after all, only "the skin on a drum beaten to achieve a calculated impact on a wider audience."[2]

Paralleling the growth in technology-driven opportunities was the effort by terrorists themselves to hone their communications skills. As one of the terrorists who orchestrated the attack on the Israeli athletes during the 1972 Munich Olympic Games testified:

We recognized that sport is the modern religion of the Western world. We knew that the people in England and America would switch their television sets from any program about the plight of the Palestinians if there was a sporting event on another channel. So we decided to use their Olympics, the most sacred ceremony of this religion, to make the world pay attention to us. We offered up human sacrifices to your gods of sport and television. And they answered our prayers.[3]

The most powerful, violent, and perfectly choreographed performance of the modern "theater of terror" was the September 11, 2001, strike on America. That November, Osama bin Laden discussed the Twin Tower attacks, referring to the suicide terrorists as "vanguards of Islam" and marveling that "those young men said in deeds, in New York and Washington, speeches that overshadowed other speeches made everywhere else in the world. The speeches are understood by both Arabs and non-Arabs, even Chinese."[4] But bin Laden's most important target audience was not the American public, but rather the inhabitants of Muslim countries. The attention conferred on him by both the mass media and political leaders elevated him to a leading global figure.

In her 2003 study, Brigitte Nacos argued that bin Laden revealed that he considered terrorism as, first and foremost, a vehicle to dispatch messages—"speeches" in his words—and he concluded that Americans, in particular, had heard and reacted with

Photo Removed Due to Copyright Restrictions

An image from a videotape posted on an Islamic Web site in September 2004, in which terrorists threaten to behead a kidnapped Western hostage.

the proper psychological impact to the intended 9/11 communication. "There is America, full of fear from north to south, from west to east," he said. "Thank God for that."[5]

By striking hard at America, Nacos argues, the terrorists took control of the global agenda, through the mass media, and changed the discussion from grieving over the thousands murdered to global exploration of their own grievances. The perpetrators had achieved, perhaps, their most important media goal: publicizing themselves, their causes, their grievances, and their demands.

The targets chosen for that event were symbols of American wealth, power, and heritage. According to a manual used in al-Qaida's training camps, publicity was—and most probably still is—an overriding consideration. Thus, jihadists were advised to target "sentimental landmarks" such as New York's Statue of Liberty, London's Big Ben, and Paris' Eiffel Tower because their destruction would "generate intense publicity."[6]

The advances in communication technology put the events of September 11 into the record books as the most watched terrorist spectacle ever.

The Terrorist Production

One of the most influential theorists of modern terrorism was the Brazilian Carlos Marighela, whose "Minimanual of the Urban Guerrilla" became a global terrorist sourcebook. He wrote:

To kidnap figures known for their artistic, sporting, or other activities who have not expressed any political views may possibly provide a form of propaganda favorable to the revolutionaries. ... Modern mass media, simply by announcing what the revolutionaries are doing, are important instruments of the propaganda. The war of nerves, or the psychological war, is a fighting technique based on the direct or indirect use of the mass media. ... Bank assaults, ambushes, desertion and diverting of arms, the rescue of prisoners, executions, kidnapping, sabotage, terrorism, and the war of nerves are all cases in point. Airplanes diverted in flight, ships and trains assaulted and seized by guerrillas, can also be solely for propaganda effects.[7]

The emergence of media-oriented terrorism has led several scholars to reconceptualize their studies: "As a symbolic act, terrorism can be analyzed much like other media of communication, consisting of four basic components: transmitter (the terrorist), intended recipient (target), message (bombing, ambush), and feedback (reaction of target audience)."[8]

Photo Removed Due to Copyright Restrictions

A member of the Arab commando group that seized and killed 11 members of the Israeli Olympic team during the 1972 summer Olympics in Munich, Germany, stands on the balcony of the Olympic village quarters where the hostages were being held.

Ralph Dowling suggested applying the concept of "rhetoric genre," arguing that "terrorists engage in recurrent rhetorical forms that force the media to provide the access without which terrorism could not fulfill its objectives."[9]

Some terrorist activities have so become what J. Bowyer Bell has called "terrorist spectaculars"[10] that they can best be analyzed as "media events." Hezbollah's attacks on Israeli targets, for example, are always taped, leading some analysts to suggest that every terror unit consists of at least four members: the perpetrator, a cameraman, a soundman, and a producer.

It is clear that terrorists plan their actions with the media as a major consideration. They select targets, location, and timing according to media preferences, trying to satisfy criteria for newsworthiness, media timetables, and deadlines. They concoct and prepare visual aides—such as film, video clips of attacks and forced "confessions" of hostages, taped interviews, and allegiance declarations of perpetrators of violence—while also offering professional press and video news releases.

Modern terrorists feed the media, both directly and indirectly, with propaganda disguised as news items. They also monitor the coverage, closely examining the reports of various journalists and their media organizations. The terrorists' pressure on reporters takes many forms—from open and friendly hosting to direct threats, blackmail, and even intimidating murders.

Finally, terrorist organizations operate their own media—from television channels (Hezbollah's Al-Manar and al-Qaida's Voice of the Caliphate), news agencies, newspapers and magazines, radio channels, and video- and audiocassettes to, most recently, Internet Web sites.

The New Arena: Terror on the Internet

Postmodern terrorists are taking advantage of the fruits of globalization and modern technology to plan, coordinate, and execute their deadly campaigns.

No longer geographically constrained within a particular territory, dependent politically or financially on a particular state, these terrorists rely on advanced communication capabilities, including the Internet, to advance their murderous agenda. In 1998, less than half of the organizations designated as Foreign Terrorist Organizations by the U.S. State Department maintained Web sites; by the end of 1999, nearly all these terrorist groups had established their presence on the Internet. Today, all active terrorist groups have established at least one presence on the Internet, with our monitoring from 1998 to 2007 revealing over 5,000 terrorist Web sites, online forums, and chat rooms.[11]

Terrorism and the Internet are related in two ways. First, the Internet has become a forum for both groups and individuals to spread messages of hate and violence and to communicate with one another, their supporters, and their sympathizers, while launching psychological warfare. Second, both individuals and groups have tried to attack computer networks in what has become known as cyber-terrorism or cyber-warfare. At this point, however, terrorists are using and benefiting from the Internet more than they are attacking it.

Computer-mediated communication is ideal for terrorists: It is decentralized, cannot be subjected to control or restriction, is not censored, and allows free access to anyone who wants it. The typical, loosely knit network of cells, divisions, and subgroups of modern terrorist organizations finds the Internet both ideal and vital for inter- and intra-group networking.

Web sites, however, are only one of the Internet's services to be hijacked by terrorists; there are many other facilities such as e-mail, chat rooms, e-groups, forums, and virtual message boards.

Many of these Web sites are used for psychological campaigns against enemy states and their military forces. They post horrifying footage of hostages and captives executed (often by primitive beheadings), and military personnel assassinated in the field by snipers, shot down by shoulder missiles, or their vehicles blown up by roadside or suicide bombers. The messages, verbal and graphic, attempt to demoralize and scare the enemy or to create feelings of guilt, doubt, and inner dissension, while delivering a threatening message to various governments and their populations. "We don't care who we kill," they say, "and none of you can be protected." They gain their power from the reaction to fear.

The Rhetoric of Terrorist Propaganda

One common element in terrorist Web sites is the justification given to the use of violence. A useful theory guiding this analysis has been Albert Bandura's theory of "moral disengagement," although not developed specifically for terrorists,[12] who, like criminals, attempt to disengage or distance themselves from their horrific use of violence, by the following methods:

- **Displacement of responsibility**—This involves distorting the relationship between one's actions and the effects of those actions, and/or blaming the victim or circumstances for violent actions and innocent deaths.

- **Diffusion of responsibility**—This is done by segmenting duties, where each individual action by itself is fairly benign, but the totality is harmful. Group decisions can also be used to diffuse individual responsibility for an action.

- **Dehumanization of targets**—Committing violence against innocents is easier if they are not perceived as fellow, individual humans. One can minimize the brutality imposed on others by focusing, instead, on the impersonal character of the attacks and the targets' symbolic meaning, and by naming and viewing the victims as less than human—vermin, dogs, and so forth. Osama bin Laden, for example, bestializes Americans as "lowly people" perpetrating acts that "the most ravenous of animals would not descend to."

- **Euphemistic language**—This includes making injurious conduct respectable and reducing personal responsibility by referring to it in impersonal terms. For example, al-Qaida always refers to the 9/11 events as attacks on symbols of American power and consumerism, never to the murder of some 3,000 men, women, and children.

- **Advantageous comparisons**—Reprehensible conduct is masked by comparing it to other, more injurious behavior. Again, the deaths of innocent

people, including children, in the 9/11 attacks during peacetime are compared to the U.S. atomic bombing of Japan to end World War II, in which hundreds of thousands were killed, but the United States was never the aggressor, not even in victory.

- **Distortion of sequence of events and attribution of blame**—Disregarding facts or distorting the consequences of a violent action on fellow citizens by arguing that a terrorist attack was only a retaliatory action or defensive measure against a previous provocation of the enemy allows terrorists to reduce personal feelings of guilt. The victim gets blamed and others are accused of bringing about reprehensible actions, as when kidnapped hostages are beheaded because their governments failed to meet terrorist demands.

An analysis of the rhetoric used on terrorist Web sites reveals that the most popular moral disengagement used is "displacement of responsibility." Violence is uniformly presented as a necessity to deal with an oppressive enemy, and all ensuing murder and destruction is attributed to others. The prime agency for jihadists engaging in terror, for example, is displaced to Allah, thereby attempting to sanitize murder and mayhem while glorifying "martyrdom."

Another rhetorical structure found on terrorist Web pages is the attempt to legitimize any members of any anti-establishment group as freedom fighters and anyone who speaks against them as "the real terrorist."

Finally, some of the sites of violent terrorist organizations are replete with the rhetoric of nonviolence, with messages claiming "love of peace," and support for a diplomatic solution. This mix of images and arguments is presented to reach all available audiences.

The Challenge Ahead

The emergence of media-oriented terrorism presents a tough challenge to democratic societies and liberal values. The threat is not limited to media manipulation and psychological warfare; it also includes the danger of restrictions imposed on the freedom of the press and expression by those who try to fight terrorism.

How should democratic societies respond? This is an extremely sensitive and delicate issue since most of the rhetoric disseminated is considered protected free speech under the U.S. Constitution or similar laws in other Western societies.

New technologies carry a paradigm shift: They empower individuals over states or societies through free access to information and mass communication. The Internet's beauty as a mass medium is in its liberal, free, and unregulated nature. Is misuse of it one of the unavoidable prices of democracy? We should be looking for a proactive compromise that will minimize its abuse by terrorists while maintaining democratic freedoms. ∎

The opinions expressed in this article do not necessarily reflect the views or policies of the U.S. government.

Endnotes

1. P. Wilkinson, *Terrorism Versus Democracy* (London: Frank Cass, 2001).

2. A. Schmid and J. de Graaf, *Violence as Communication* (Beverly Hills, CA: Sage, 1982).

3. C. Dobson and R. Paine. *The Carlos Complex: A Pattern of Violence* (London: Hodder and Stoughton, 1977).

4. The quotes are taken from the translations of a videotape, presumably made in mid-November 2001 in Afghanistan. Available at *http://www.washingtonpost.com/wp-srv/nation/specials.*

5. B. Nacos, "The Terrorist Calculus Behind 9-11: A Model for Future Terrorism?" *Studies in Conflict and Terrorism,* vol. 26 (2003): pp. 1–16.

6. Hamza Hendawi, "Terror Manual Advises on Targets." Available at *http://story.news.yahoo.com/news?tmpl=story&u+/ap/20.../afghan_spreading_terror_*

7. C. Marighela, "Minimanual of the Urban Guerrilla," in J. Mallin (ed.), *Terror and the Urban Guerrilla* (Coral Gables, FL: University of Miami Press, 1971).

8. P. Karber, "Urban Terrorism: Baseline Data and a Conceptual Framework," *Social Science Quarterly*, vol. 52 (1971): pp. 527-533.

9. R.E. Dowling, "Terrorism and the Media: A Rhetorical Genre," *Journal of Communication*, vol. 56, no. 1 (1986): pp. 12-24.

10. J.B. Bell, "Terrorist Script and Live-Action Spectaculars," *Columbia Journalism Review* (May-June 1978): pp. 47-50.

11. Gabriel Weimann, *WWW.Terror.Net: How Modern Terrorism Uses the Internet* (special report) (Washington D.C.: United States Institute of Peace, 2004); Gabriel Weimann, *Terror on the Internet: The New Arena, The New Challenges* (Washington, D.C.: United States Institute of Peace, 2006); Gabriel Weimann, "Virtual Disputes: The Use of the Internet for Terrorist Debates," *Studies in Conflict and Terrorism*, vol. 29, no. 7 (2006): pp. 623-639.

12. A. Bandura, "Moral Disengagement in the Perpetration of Inhumanities," *Personality and Social Psychology Review* (special issue on evil and violence), vol. 3 (1999): pp. 193–209; A. Bandura, "Selective Moral Disengagement in the Exercise of Moral Agency," *Journal of Moral Education*, vol. 31, no. 2 (2002): pp. 101-119; and A. Bandura, "The Role of Selective Moral Disengagement in Terrorism and Counterterrorism," in F. M. Moghaddam and A. J. Marsella (eds), *Understanding Terrorism: Psychological Roots, Consequences and Interventions* (Washington, D.C.: American Psychological Association, 2004), pp 121-150.

A Case Study:
The Mythology of Martyrdom in Iraq
Mohammed M. Hafez

Photo Removed Due to Copyright Restrictions

Iraqi Special Operations Forces demonstrate their ability to fight terrorists at a graduation ceremony attended by the U.S. commander in Iraq, General David H. Petraeus, and Iraqi Prime Minister Nouri al-Maliki.

Mohammed M. Hafez, PhD, a visiting professor in the Department of Political Science at the University of Missouri in Kansas City, recently released his latest book, Suicide Bombers in Iraq: The Strategy and Ideology of Martyrdom, *published by the U.S. Institute of Peace.*

Jihadists in Iraq confront a challenging communication problem. Their messages must achieve five goals: appeal to potential recruits inside and outside of Iraq; justify to the public the killing of civilians and fellow Muslims in insurgent attacks; deactivate self-inhibiting norms that may obstruct their cadres from killing civilians in suicide attacks; legitimize the organizations that engage in violence; and counter the claims of authorities in Iraq and around the Muslim world.

They formulate a number of utilitarian, ideological, and theological arguments to achieve these tasks. However, to avoid overwhelming their audiences with information and complicated discourse, jihadists simplify their message by relying on emotional narratives that construct the image of the "heroic martyr."

Through online video clips and biographies of suicide bombers, they play on themes of humiliation, collusion, and redemption to demonize their enemies and motivate their cadres to make "heroic" sacrifices. They exaggerate mistreatment of women and appeal to the masculinity of men in order to shame them into protecting their "mothers and sisters." These emotive elements are intended to galvanize support, not just from a narrow circle of activists but also from the broader Muslim public.

The dominant narratives revolve around three themes that are often presented in a sequence, as if to show a play in three acts.

- Act One depicts the humiliation and suffering of Muslims in Iraq and elsewhere, and suggests that there is a conspiracy by Western "crusaders" to target Muslims.
- Act Two is designed to show existing Muslim regimes as impotent and in collusion with the West, suggesting that they are not the true leaders of the Muslim world, but servants of their Western "masters."
- Act Three insists on the inevitability of Muslim victory because the "pious and heroic" have stepped forward to redeem the suffering and humiliation of their fellow Muslims through faith in God, sacrifice on the battlefield, and righteousness in their cause.

These three narratives are sometimes presented separately, but often they are woven together to suggest a problem, the cause, and a solution.

This article explores martyrdom mythologies in Iraq by drawing extensively on the literature of jihadists since the beginning of the Iraqi insurgency. These include video clips, audio recordings, biographies of suicide bombers, online magazines, and still images posted online. Special emphasis is given to how jihadists portray the fallen "martyrs." By elevating the suicide bombers to the status of extraordinary moral beings who make the ultimate sacrifice for God and the Muslim nation, jihadists deflect attention away from the atrocities they commit and the victims they harm.

It must be made clear from the outset that the portrayal of bombers in video clips and biographies is highly propagandistic. The point of focusing on martyrdom mythologies is to show how groups seek to achieve several communication goals through manipulation of narratives, not to suggest that these mythologies reflect the truth.

The Context

Since 2003, the number of suicide bombings in Iraq has surpassed all those of Hamas in Israel, Hezbollah in Lebanon, and the Tamil Tigers in Sri Lanka combined. The overwhelming majority targeted Iraqi security forces and Shiite civilians, not Coalition forces. Many, if not most, of the perpetrators of these suicide bombings are non-Iraqi volunteers. Most are connected to jihadi networks associated with "second-generation" jihadists who trained in Afghanistan during the 1990s, militants fleeing arrest in their home or host countries, and new recruits enraged by the suffering of Muslims in Iraq.

The Iraqi insurgents rely on a diverse tool kit of tactics, the most deadly being improvised explosive devices (IEDs) and car bombs driven by suicide bombers. However, insurgents also intimidate "collaborators," such as translators and manual laborers employed by the Coalition forces; sabotage electric stations, oil and water pipelines and facilities, and reconstruction projects; lob improvised rockets and mortar shells at Coalition positions and fire surface-to-air rockets at airplanes and helicopters; kidnap local citizens and foreigners to exchange them for ransom or execute them, as well as kidnap members of the security services and "spies" to interrogate and execute them; and carry out suicide attacks using explosive vests.

Insurgents also attack international organizations such as the United Nations, nongovernmental agencies such as the Red Cross, and representatives of foreign governments. They have attacked the Jordanian and Turkish embassies and killed Algerian, Egyptian, and Russian diplomats.

Photo Removed Due to Copyright Restrictions

Iraqi soldiers inspect a van destroyed in an attack in Baqouba, Iraq, in April 2007. The suicide bomber killed a 12-year-old boy and wounded another nine civilians.

Family members of 18 children who died in a car bomb attack in a Shiite neighborhood of Baghdad sit with portraits of their children during a commemoration luncheon with Iraqi government officials in July 2005.

There is a strategic logic to why insurgents attack the targets they do. Expansive violence is intended to create widespread insecurity among the public, engender sectarian polarization, and produce economic collapse. All of these outcomes delegitimize the new order; allow the insurgents to portray themselves as the sole protectors of Sunnis, thus being able to command their support; and create a failed state whereby the central authority does not have a monopoly on the use of coercive force, which allows jihadists, with an agenda beyond Iraq, to establish a base for operations, recruitment, and training.

Justifications for Suicide Attacks

Al-Qaida in Iraq had declared responsibility for 30 percent of the claimed suicide attacks in Iraq as of February 2006. Since October 2006, the Islamic State of Iraq, set up as a front organization for al-Qaida in Iraq, has claimed responsibility for nearly all suicide attacks there.

Abu Dujana al-Ansari, the head of al-Qaida's al-Bara Bin Malik Brigade (suicide bombing squad), justifies suicide attacks against "the strongest and most advanced army in modern times" in a montage dedicated to Abu Musab al-Zarqawi, the killed terrorist leader. Al-Ansari says that the suicide brigade was created following the earlier advice of Osama bin Laden to terrorize the enemy and penetrate its defenses in order to demoralize its soldiers.

But how do they justify attacking fellow Muslims? Insurgents in Iraq, not just those associated with al-Qaida, answer that the Iraqi security forces are a mere

extension of the occupation forces. Further, al-Qaida argues that Shiite militias attack, torture, and kill Sunnis; abuse and humiliate them at checkpoints; and serve as spies for the occupation forces. Many of their videos are dedicated to this theme. In justifying attacks against the ruling Iraqi officials, the nationalists and Salafi jihadi insurgents argue that this is an illegitimate government—indeed, a puppet regime—that came to power with the help of enemies and rules only because the Coalition forces allow it to, despite the democratic election process.

Secularism, nationalism, and Shiism are portrayed as instruments of a nefarious plot led by "crusaders" and "Zionists." The jihadist arguments are: Secularism, they say, divides the world into religious and nonreligious spheres, which is antithetical to Islam as a violation of God's sovereignty over right and wrong, permissible and forbidden; nationalism, in turn, fosters narrow identifications with language, land, and borders, not a broader unity among the community of Muslim faithful; and Shiism, the jihadists claim, gives ascendancy to a heretical creed, and Shiites are presented as the most dangerous tool against the true believers because they "appear" Islamic, but, in jihadist reality, loathe the people of the Sunna and wait for the opportunity to betray them.

These ideological justifications are intended for a narrow milieu of committed jihadists who may question certain tactics or targets of the insurgents, especially when it comes to indiscriminate attacks on fellow Muslims. To the extent that these highly controversial arguments are produced for the wider Muslim public, they are usually accompanied by vivid imagery and emotional narratives that shock the moral conscience of Muslims, demonize the Shiites and Iraqi security forces, and heighten the sense of threat to Muslims worldwide.

Insurgents in Iraq do not depend solely on the force of ideology in mobilizing support for martyrdom. They also seek to cut across ideological and political divides by appealing to emotional and personal themes embedded in the culture and ethos of Arabs and Muslims. Their narratives rely on three themes: humiliation, impotence due to collusion, and redemption through faith and sacrifice.

Humiliation

At the heart of the narratives is the theme of humiliation at the hands of callous and arrogant powers. Images of collective humiliation often begin with footage from the initial phase of the combat in Iraq in 2003, depicting the asymmetry in power and showing emotional photographs of destroyed mosques, bloodied victims, and house searches. These and, above all, images from Abu Ghraib prison personalize the suffering and heighten the sense of powerlessness and indignation that many Muslims feel.

Images from Iraq are usually combined with those from other conflicts in Muslim areas, especially Palestine. The intent is to deliver two messages. The first is that the suffering and humiliation of Muslims around the world are not unconnected episodes, but a chain of transgressions by a "crusader-Zionist alliance." This message heightens the sense of threat in order to justify extraordinary measures to fight the conspiracy against Islam.

The second message is that Iraq is the central battlefield in which to wage war against the enemies of Islam. Fighting in Iraq, in effect, is the same as fighting in Palestine, Chechnya, Kashmir, Saudi Arabia, and elsewhere in the Muslim world, as, to the jihadists, these are all one struggle, not separate wars. In framing the conflict in this light, insurgents can call on jihadists everywhere to come to Iraq, claiming that a victory there is victory in every Muslim land.

Jihadists also rely heavily on the theme of female dishonor and suffering at the hands of foreigners and Iraqi security forces. Images of women terrified as soldiers storm into their homes to search for insurgents, videos of women being frisked, rumors of women abducted or taken into custody where they are humiliated or worse, and stories of women being handed over by Iraqi forces as hostages to be exchanged for wanted insurgents are replete in jihadists narratives. Undoubtedly, these are appealing to notions of masculinity that pervade tribal culture, in which *sharaf* (nobleness), `*ird* (honor), and *muruah* (chivalry or manliness) are of vital importance. These notions of masculinity are often judged by one's zealous protection of and control over women so they do not risk straying in their relations with men and, therefore, bring shame to the entire family or tribe.

Impotence and Collusion

Part of the narrative is to show the "arrogance" of Coalition forces and the alleged collusion of Muslim governments. Insurgent videos often use the clip of President George W. Bush on board a U.S. aircraft carrier declaring victory in Iraq. This is usually followed by footage of U.S. troops marching in the streets of Iraq or walking through Saddam Hussein's palaces. Occasionally, one sees the famous image of a U.S. soldier placing the American flag atop Saddam's statue in Baghdad.

Following closely are images showing Arab leaders— King Abdullah in Saudi Arabia, King Abdullah II in Jordan, Hosni Mubarak in Egypt, and the post-invasion Iraqi leadership (Iyad Alawi, Ibrahim al-Jaafari, Jalal Talabani, and Abdel Aziz al-Hakim, among others) in the company of Coalition officials, President Bush, and British Prime Minister Tony Blair. These leaders are smiling and sometimes embracing. Other images include Arab and/or Western leaders in the company of Israeli leaders, especially a 2004 photo of President Bush shaking hands with former Israeli Prime Minister Ariel Sharon in the White House during the al-Aqsa uprising, also known as the second *intifada* (2000-2005).

This imagery is important for five reasons:
- First, it portrays anyone working for the government in Iraq as in collusion with the West. Those who persist in this collusion, then, are fair game and can be killed without moral compunction.
- Second, by identifying these leaders as "puppets" working for foreign powers, their moral criticism of the jihadists and their tactics are without force—who are they to challenge the legitimacy of the insurgents?
- Third, portraying these governments as impotent explains the necessity for other Muslims to step forward to fight in their stead. Jihad, then, becomes an individual obligation (*fard_'ayn*) because the existing governments have supposedly abdicated their duty toward protecting Muslim lands and liberating them from unbelievers.
- Fourth, illustrating that jihadists do not have the support or resources of official governments justifies their demands for extraordinary measures and calls for martyrdom.
- Finally, these images frame the struggle in Iraq in broader terms than simply liberating that country from a foreign occupation. Instead, it is represented as a struggle to replace all the "corrupt" and "mercenary" regimes that currently rule in the Muslim world with ones that are truly Islamic.

Photo Removed Due to Copyright Restrictions

This victim of a suicide bomber is being taken to a hospital in northern Iraq in Febraury 2004. At least 57 people were killed and more than 250 wounded in the attack.

Redemption Through Faith and Sacrifice

Acts One and Two can be disempowering if not followed by Act Three, which presents the solution: salvation and redemption of all Muslims through faith in God and a desire to sacrifice in His path.

An important element in Act Three is the mythology surrounding martyrdom and martyrs. Al-Qaida in Iraq promotes the image of a heroic Muslim willing to make the ultimate sacrifice to redeem his nation and avenge the personal suffering inflicted on helpless Muslims, especially women. The propaganda surrounding the "martyrs" is issued on Web postings, videos of operations, and in al-Qaida's online journal entitled *Biographies of Eminent Martyrs.*

These productions—often short, inconsistent in the information they present, and highly propagandistic—reveal at least four themes that make up the mythology of martyrdom:

- Sincere devotion to religion
- Willingness to sacrifice one's wealth and personal ties for God
- Eagerness to carry out a "martyrdom operation"
- Success in sacrifice operations

Sincere devotion to Islam: Insurgent videos are replete with images of pious Muslims praying, chanting "God is great" (*allahu akbar*), even as they are in the midst of an operation, such as planting an IED. Suicide bombers, in particular, are almost invariably portrayed as deeply religious people. The biographies often detail at length how the "martyr" prayed incessantly, spent his time reading or memorizing the Quran, and went beyond religious obligations in voluntary expressions of devotion.

The emphasis on sincerity in devotion is important because suicide bombings can be considered martyrdom only if the individual bombers are adherent Muslims fighting out of faith in God and dying for His sake. One cannot expect to receive the rewards of martyrdom if he or she is motivated by something other than love of God and striving in His path. Perhaps more importantly, jihadi Salafis are aware that Muslim governments attempt to portray jihadists as "deviants" and misguided individuals who know little about Islam and have been brainwashed into carrying out suicide attacks. Stressing the religiosity of the bombers, therefore, is al-Qaida's attempt to counter those claims.

Willingness to sacrifice personal wealth and family ties: The propaganda of al-Qaida portrays the "martyrs" as people who have given up all things dear in order to fulfill a higher obligation: jihad and martyrdom. They claim that many of the bombers are from wealthy families or have made personal sacrifices, such as selling their cars, using their meager savings, or relying on donations to make the trip to Iraq. Many biographies make use of the powerful imagery of a father leaving his newborn child or a husband leaving his wife to fight and die in the path of God.

These narratives are intended to inspire others and set a new standard for devotion to the faith. They demand that, to be a good Muslim, it is not enough to pray regularly and carry out one's ritual obligations. One must also exert as much effort as necessary to reach and die for the land of jihad.

Eagerness to conduct a "martyrdom operation": Again and again, we read in the biographies that the "martyrs" are eager to die in the path of God and are frustrated when denied or delayed. Almost every clip shows

Photo Removed Due to Copyright Restrictions

In August 2004 on its Web site, the Ansar Al-Sunna Army claimed that this was one of 12 Nepalese workers kidnapped in Iraq.

the bombers as happy: They usually wave goodbye with smiles on their faces as they run toward their explosive-laden vehicles, reflecting the theme of joy in sacrifice and assurance of the rewards they will earn in paradise.

This theme of eagerness and joy is intended to show that the bombers are neither coerced nor brainwashed into carrying out suicide attacks. Iraqi satellite channels, however, often air "confessions" of foiled bombers who claim that they did not know that they were about to engage in a suicide operation, because someone else was in control of the detonator while they thought they were merely delivering the truck to the target. Some are said to have had their hands handcuffed to the steering wheel and others claim to have been given drugs and shown pornographic materials, to excite them into meeting heavenly maidens. The theme of eagerness to die, therefore, is intended to dispel these allegations and elevate the status of the suicide bombers to faithful and heroic martyrs fully in control of their choices and destinies.

Success in martyrdom operations: Invariably, the biographies of the martyrs emphasize, or more often exaggerate, the success of suicide missions as if to assure potential recruits that their worldly sacrifices will not be in vain. The number of "apostates," "crusaders," and "CIA agents" claimed to be killed in individual operations are often in the hundreds. One finds repeatedly claims that the bombers killed more than is reported in the media, which

"rely on American numbers." One often hears that the Americans dump their dead in rivers or in hastily prepared graves to cover up their real losses. Given their "success," the biographers term each operation as "conquest" (*ghazwah*), such as *ghazwit al-Nasiriyah* (the attack on Italian forces in Nasiriyah, which killed 31 people). The term *ghazwah* is an intentional allusion to battles in early Islamic history, when Muslims fought and ultimately triumphed over the unbelievers.

Understanding the Ploys

Martyrdom mythologies are not sufficient to explain all the suicide bombings in Iraq. However, ideology, religious framing, and emotional narratives help explain how jihadists deactivate self-inhibiting norms against murder and mayhem and allow them to appear as moral agents even when they are acting in immoral ways.

Justifications for killing fellow Muslims are anchored in emotional, poignant narratives that link suffering and humiliation of Muslims to what is portrayed as the collusion of impotent Muslim leaders and their agents with Western oppressors, who, the extremists claim, are seeking to destroy Islam and subjugate Muslim lands. By framing the struggle in those terms, the jihadists make it appear logical that a "heroic" cadre is needed to step forward, redeem the honor of the nation, and erase the shame of humiliation by striking at those who work with the enemy.

Understanding these ploys is an important step to combating terrorism. ∎

The opinions expressed in this article do not necessarily reflect the views or policies of the U.S. government.

New Paradigms for 21st-Century Conflict

David J. Kilcullen

Photo Removed Due to Copyright Restrictions

The multinational force monitoring the ceasefire following the 2006 war between Israel and Hezbollah is an example of recent cooperation among the international community to address the new types of conflict that have arisen in the 21st century. Here, U.N. Secretary-General Ban Ki-moon thanks the men and women from the 30 countries participating in this effort.

David J. Kilcullen, PhD, a former Australian Army lieutenant colonel, is currently senior counterinsurgency adviser to the commanding general, Multi-National Force - Iraq. He previously served as chief strategist in the U.S. Department of State's Office of the Coordinator for Counterterrorism and as the Pentagon's special adviser for irregular warfare and counterterrorism on the 2006 Quadrennial Defense Review. *He regularly contributes to the* Small War Journal Blog. *This paper, like his postings, solely reflects his personal views.*

Despite our rather rosy hindsight view of World War II, there was considerable dissent at the time about the war's aims, conduct, and strategy. But virtually no one disagreed that it was indeed a war or that the Axis powers were the enemy/aggressors.

Contrast this with the war on terrorism. Some dispute the notion that the conflict can be defined as a war; others question the reality of the threat. Far-left critics blame American industrial interests, while a lunatic fringe sees September 11, 2001, as a massive self-inflicted conspiracy. More seriously, people disagree about the enemy. Is al-Qaida a real threat or a creature of Western paranoia and overreaction? Is it even a real organization? Is al-Qaida a mass movement or simply a philosophy, a state of mind? Is the enemy all terrorism? Is it extremism? Or is Islam itself in some way a threat? Is this primarily a military, political, or civilizational problem? What would "victory" look like? These fundamentals are disputed, as those of previous conflicts (except possibly the Cold War) were not.

In truth, the al-Qaida threat is all too real. But ambiguity arises because this conflict breaks existing paradigms—including notions of "warfare," "diplomacy," "intelligence," and even "terrorism." How, for example, do we wage war on nonstate actors who hide in states with which we are at peace? How do we work with allies whose territory provides safe haven for nonstate opponents? How do we defeat enemies who exploit the tools of globalization and open societies, without destroying the very things we seek to protect?

A New Paradigm

British General Rupert Smith argues that war—defined as industrial, interstate warfare between armies, where the clash of arms decides the outcome—no longer exists, that we are instead in an era of "war amongst the people," where the utility of military forces depends on their ability to adapt to complex political contexts and engage nonstate opponents under the critical gaze of global public opinion.[1] Certainly, in complex, multisided, irregular conflicts such as Iraq, conventional warfare has failed to produce decisive outcomes. We have instead adopted policing, nation-building, and counterinsurgency approaches—and developed new interagency tools "on the fly."

Similarly, we traditionally conduct state-based diplomacy through engagement with elites of other societies: governments, intelligentsia, and business leaders, among others. The theory is that problems can be resolved when elites agree, cooler heads prevail, and governments negotiate and then enforce agreements. Notions of sovereignty, the nation-state, treaty regimes, and international institutions all build on this paradigm. Yet the enemy organizes at the nonelite level, exploiting discontent and alienation across numerous countries, to aggregate the effects of multiple grassroots actors into a mass movement with global reach. How do elite models of diplomacy address that challenge? This is not a new problem—various programs were established in U.S. embassies in the Cold War to engage with nongovernmental elements of civil societies at risk from Communist subversion. But many such programs lapsed after 1992, and problems of religious extremism or political violence require subtly different approaches.

Likewise, traditional intelligence services are not primarily designed to find out what is happening but to acquire secrets from other nation-states. They are well-adapted to state-based targets but less suited to nonstate actors—where the problem is to acquire information that is unclassified but located in denied, hostile, or inaccessible physical or human terrain. Even against state actors, traditional intelligence cannot tell us what is happening, only what other governments believe is happening. Why, for example, did Western intelligence miss the imminent fall of the Soviet Union in 1992? In part, because we were reading the Soviet leaders' mail—and they themselves failed to understand the depth of grassroots disillusionment with Communism.[2] Why did most countries (including those that opposed the Iraq war) believe in 2002 that Saddam Hussein's regime had weapons of mass destruction? Because they were intercepting the regime's communications, and many senior Iraqi regime members believed Iraq had them.[3]

Long-standing trends underpin this environment. Drivers include globalization and the backlash against it, the rise of nonstate actors with capabilities comparable to some nation-states, U.S. conventional military superiority

that forces all opponents to avoid its strengths and migrate toward unconventional approaches, and a global information environment based on the Internet and satellite communications. All these trends would endure even if al-Qaida disappeared tomorrow, and until we demonstrate an ability to defeat this type of threat, any smart adversary will adopt a similar approach. Far from being a one-off challenge, we may look back on al-Qaida as the harbinger of a new era of conflict.

Adapting to the New Environment

Thus, as former U.S. Counterterrorism Ambassador Hank Crumpton observed, we seem to be on the threshold of a new era of warfare, one that demands an adaptive response. Like dinosaurs outcompeted by smaller, weaker, but more adaptive mammals, in this new era, nation-states are more powerful but less agile and flexible than nonstate opponents. As in all conflict, success will depend on our ability to adapt, evolve new responses, and get ahead of a rapidly changing threat environment.

Photo Removed Due to Copyright Restrictions

The names of U.S. government agencies engaged in the fight against terrorism are displayed during a hearing on federal reorganization to combat terrorism in June 2002.

The enemy adapts with great speed. Consider al-Qaida's evolution since the mid-1990s. Early attacks (the East African embassy bombings, the USS *Cole*, and 9/11 itself) were "expeditionary": Al-Qaida formed a team in Country A, prepared it in Country B, and clandestinely infiltrated it into Country C to attack a target. In response, we improved transportation security, infrastructure protection, and immigration controls. In turn, terrorists developed a "guerrilla" approach where, instead of building a team remotely and inserting it secretly to attack, they

Five Practical Steps

In responding to this counterintuitive form of warfare, the United States has done two basic things so far. First, we improved existing institutions (through processes like intelligence reform, creation of the Department of Homeland Security, and additional capacity for "irregular"—that is, nontraditional—warfare within the Department of Defense). Second, we have begun developing new paradigms to fit the new reality. These are yet to fully emerge, though some—such as the idea of treating the conflict as a very large-scale counterinsurgency problem, requiring primarily nonmilitary responses coupled with measures to protect at-risk populations from enemy influence—have gained traction.[5]

But in a sense, policy makers today are a little like the "Chateau Generals" of the First World War—confronting a form of conflict that invalidates received wisdom, just as the generals faced the "riddle of the trenches" in 1914-1918. Like them, we face a conflict environment transformed by new technological and social conditions, for which existing organizations and concepts are ill-suited. Like them, we have "work-arounds," but have yet to develop the breakthrough concepts, technologies, and organizations—equivalent to *blitzkrieg* in the 1930s—that would solve the riddle of this new threat environment.

There is no easy answer (if there were, we would have found it by now), but it is possible to suggest a way forward. This involves three conceptual steps to develop new models and, simultaneously, two organizational steps to create a capability for this form of conflict. This is not meant to be prescriptive, but is simply one possible approach. And the ideas put forward are not particularly original—rather, this proposal musters existing ideas and integrates them into a policy approach.

1. Develop a new lexicon: Professor Michael Vlahos has pointed out that the language we use to describe the new threats actively hinders innovative thought.[6] Our terms draw on negative formulations; they say what the environment is not, rather than what it is. These terms include descriptors like *un*conventional, *non*state,

Photo Removed Due to Copyright Restrictions

In a warehouse on the outskirts of the Jordanian capital of Amman, workers store blankets donated by the U.S. Agency for International Development for distribution in Iraq.

grew the team close to the target using nationals of the host country. The Madrid and London bombings, and attacks in Casablanca, Istanbul, and Jeddah, followed this pattern, as did the foiled London airline plot of summer 2006.

These attacks are often described as "home grown," yet they were inspired, exploited, and to some extent directed by al-Qaida. For example, Mohammed Siddeque Khan, leader of the July 7, 2005, London attack, flew to Pakistan and probably met al-Qaida representatives for guidance and training well before the bombing.[4] But the new approach temporarily invalidated our countermeasures—instead of smuggling 19 people in, the terrorists brought one man out—side-stepping our new security procedures. The terrorists had adapted to our new approach by evolving new techniques of their own.

We are now, of course, alert to this "guerrilla" method, as the failure of the August 2006 plots in the United Kingdom and other recent potential attacks showed. But terrorists are undoubtedly already developing new adaptive measures. In counterterrorism, methods that work are almost by definition already obsolete: Our opponents evolve as soon as we master their current approach. There is no "silver bullet." Similar to malaria, terrorism constantly morphs into new mutations that require a continuously updated battery of responses.

*non*traditional, *un*orthodox, and *ir*regular. Terminology undoubtedly influences our ability to think clearly. One reason why planners in Iraq may have treated "major combat operations" (Phase III) as decisive, not realizing that in this case the post-conflict phase would actually be critical, is that Phase III is decisive by definition. Its full doctrinal name is "Phase III—Decisive Operations." To think clearly about new threats, we need a new lexicon based on the actual, observed characteristics of real enemies who:

- Integrate terrorism, subversion, humanitarian work, and insurgency to support propaganda designed to manipulate the perceptions of local and global audiences

- Aggregate the effects of a very large number of grassroots actors, scattered across many countries, into a mass movement greater than the sum of its parts, with dispersed leadership and planning functions that deny us detectable targets

- Exploit the speed and ubiquity of modern communications media to mobilize supporters and sympathizers, at speeds far greater than governments can muster

- Exploit deep-seated belief systems founded in religious, ethnic, tribal, or cultural identity, to create extremely lethal, nonrational reactions among social groups

- Exploit safe havens such as ungoverned or undergoverned areas (in physical or cyber space); ideological, religious, or cultural blind spots; or legal loopholes

- Use high-profile symbolic attacks that provoke nation-states into overreactions that damage their long-term interests

- Mount numerous, cheap, small-scale challenges to exhaust us by provoking expensive containment, prevention, and response efforts in dozens of remote areas

These features of the new environment could generate a lexicon to better describe the threat. Since the new threats are not state-based, the basis for our approach should not be international relations (the study of how nation-states interact in elite state-based frameworks) but anthropology (the study of social roles, groups, status, institutions, and relations within human population groups, in nonelite, nonstate-based frameworks).

2. Get the grand strategy right: If this confrontation is based on long-standing trends, it follows that it may be a protracted, generational, or multigenerational struggle.

This means we need both a "long view" and a "broad view"[7] that consider how best to interweave all strands of national power, including the private sector and the wider community. Thus we need a grand strategy that can be sustained by the American people, successive U.S. administrations, key allies, and partners worldwide. Formulating such a long-term grand strategy would involve four crucial judgments:

- Deciding whether our interests are best served by intervening in and trying to mitigate the process of political and religious ferment in the Muslim world, or by seeking instead to contain any spillover of violence or unrest into Western communities. This choice is akin to that between "rollback" and "containment" in the Cold War and is a key element in framing a long-term response.

- Deciding how to allocate resources among military and nonmilitary elements of national power. Our present spending and effort are predominantly military; by contrast, a "global counterinsurgency" approach would suggest that about 80 percent of effort should go toward political, diplomatic, development, intelligence, and informational activity, and about 20 percent to military activity. Whether this is appropriate depends on our judgment about intervention versus containment.

- Deciding how much to spend (in resources and lives) on this problem. This will require a risk judgment taking into account the likelihood and consequences of future terrorist attacks. Such a judgment must also consider how much can be spent on security without imposing an unsustainable cost burden on our societies.

- Deciding how to prioritize effort geographically. At present most effort goes to Iraq, a much smaller portion to Afghanistan, and less again to all other areas. Partly this is because our spending is predominantly military and because we have chosen to intervene in the heart of the Muslim world. Different choices on the military/nonmilitary and intervention/containment judgments might produce significantly different regional priorities over time.

Clearly, the specifics of any administration's strategy would vary in response to a developing situation. Indeed, such agility is critical. But achieving a sustainable consensus, nationally and internationally, on the four grand judgments listed above, would provide a long-term basis for policy across successive administrations.

3. Remedy the imbalance in government capability: At present, the U.S. defense budget accounts for approximately half of total global defense spending, while the U.S. armed forces employ about 1.68 million uniformed members.[8] By comparison, the State Department employs about 6,000 foreign service officers, while the U.S. Agency for International Development (USAID) has about 2,000.[9] In other words, the Department of Defense is about 210 times larger than USAID and State combined—there are substantially more people employed as musicians in Defense bands than in the entire foreign service.[10]

This is not to criticize Defense—armed services are labor- and capital-intensive and are always larger than diplomatic or aid agencies. But considering the importance, in this form of conflict, of development, diplomacy, and information (the U.S. Information Agency was abolished in 1999 and the State Department figures given include its successor bureau), a clear imbalance exists between military and nonmilitary elements of capacity. This distorts policy and is unusual by global standards. For example, Australia's military is approximately nine times larger than its diplomatic and aid agencies combined: The military arm is larger, but not 210 times larger, than the other elements of national power.

To its credit, the Department of Defense recognizes the problems inherent in such an imbalance, and said so in the 2006 *Quadrennial Defense Review*.[11] And the Bush administration has programs in train to increase nonmilitary capacity. But to succeed over the long haul, we need a sustained commitment to build nonmilitary elements of national power. So-called soft powers, such as private-sector economic strength, national reputation, and cultural confidence, are crucial, because military power

Photo Removed Due to Copyright Restrictions

Soldiers from many nations, including these Indonesian commandos who are applauding their colleagues during an anti-terror exercise conducted outside Jakarta in 2006, have joined in the international fight against terrorism.

alone cannot compensate for their loss.

These three conceptual steps will take time (which is, incidentally, a good reason to start on them). But in the interim, two organizational steps could prepare the way:

4. Identify the new "strategic services": A leading role in the war on terrorism has fallen to Special Operations Forces (SOF) because of their direct action capabilities against targets in remote or denied areas. Meanwhile, Max Boot[12] has argued that we again need something like the Office of Strategic Services (OSS) of World War II, which included analysis, intelligence, anthropology, special operations, information, psychological operations, and technology capabilities.

Adjectives matter: Special Forces versus Strategic Services. SOF are special. They are defined by internal comparison to the rest of the military—SOF undertake tasks "beyond the capabilities" of general-purpose forces. By contrast, OSS was strategic. It was defined against an external environment and undertook tasks of strategic importance, rapidly acquiring and divesting capabilities as needed. SOF are almost entirely military; OSS was an interagency body with a sizeable civilian component, and almost all its military personnel were emergency war enlistees (talented civilians with strategically relevant skills, enlisted for the duration of the war).[13] SOF trace their origin to OSS; yet whereas today's SOF are elite military forces with highly specialized capabilities optimized for seven standard missions,[14] OSS was a mixed civil-military organization that took whatever mission the environment demanded, building capabilities as needed.

Identifying which capabilities are strategic services today would be a key step in prioritizing interagency efforts. Capabilities for dealing with nonelite, grassroots threats include cultural and ethnographic intelligence, social systems analysis, information operations (see below), early-entry or high-threat humanitarian and governance teams, field negotiation and mediation teams, biometric reconnaissance, and a variety of other strategically relevant capabilities. The relevance of these capabilities changes over time—some that are strategically relevant now would cease to be, while others would emerge. The key is the creation of an interagency capability to rapidly acquire and apply techniques and technologies in a fast-changing situation.

Photo Removed Due to Copyright Restrictions

A U.S. national guardsman works with an Iraqi police officer at the Major Crime Unit in western Baghdad..

5. Develop a capacity for strategic information warfare: Al-Qaida is highly skilled at exploiting multiple, diverse actions by individuals and groups, by framing them in a propaganda narrative to manipulate local and global audiences. Al-Qaida maintains a network that collects information about the debate in the West and feeds this, along with an assessment of the effectiveness of al-Qaida's propaganda, to its leaders. They use physical operations (bombings, insurgent activity, beheadings) as supporting material for an integrated "armed propaganda" campaign. The "information" side of al-Qaida's operation is primary; the physical is merely the tool to achieve a propaganda result. The Taliban, GSPC (previously, the Salafist Group for Preaching and Combat, now known as al-Qaida in the Islamic Maghreb), and some other al-Qaida-aligned groups, as well as Hezbollah, adopt similar approaches.

Contrast this with our approach: We typically design physical operations first, then craft supporting information operations to explain our actions. This is the reverse of al-Qaida's approach. For all our professionalism, compared to the enemy's, our public information is an afterthought. In military terms, for al-Qaida the "main effort" is information; for us, information is a "supporting effort." As noted, there are 1.68 million people in the U.S. military, and what they do speaks louder than what our public information professionals (who number in the hundreds) say. Thus, to combat extremist propaganda, we need a capacity for strategic information warfare—an integrating function that draws together all components of what we say and what we do to send strategic messages that support our overall policy.

At present, the military has a well-developed information operations doctrine, but other agencies do not, and they are often rightly wary of military methods. Militarizing information operations would be a severe mistake that would confuse a part (military operations) with the whole (U.S. national strategy) and so undermine our overall policy. Lacking a whole-of-government doctrine and the capability to fight strategic information warfare limits our effectiveness and creates message dissonance, in which different elements of the U.S. government send out different messages or work to differing information agendas.

We need an interagency effort, with leadership from the very top in the executive and legislative branches of government, to create capabilities, organizations, and doctrine for a national-level strategic information campaign. Building such a capability is perhaps the most important of our many capability challenges in this new era of information-driven conflict.

Tentative Conclusions

These notions—a new lexicon, grand strategy, balanced capability, strategic services, and strategic information warfare—are merely speculative ideas that suggest what might emerge from a comprehensive effort to find new paradigms for this new era of conflict. Different ideas may well emerge from such an effort, and, in any case, rapid changes in the environment due to enemy adaptation will demand constant innovation. But it is crystal clear that our traditional paradigms of industrial interstate war, elite-based diplomacy, and state-focused intelligence can no longer explain the environment or provide conceptual keys to overcome today's threats.

The Cold War is a limited analogy for today's conflict: There are many differences between today's threats and those of the Cold War era. Yet in at least one dimension, that of time, the enduring trends that drive the current confrontation may mean that the conflict will indeed resemble the Cold War, which lasted in one form or another for the 75 years between the Russian Revolution in 1917 and the collapse of the Soviet Union in December 1991. Many of its consequences—especially the "legacy conflicts" arising from the Soviet-Afghan War—are with us still. Even if this confrontation lasts only half as long as the Cold War, we are at the beginning of a very long road indeed, whether we choose to recognize it or not.

The new threats, which invalidate received wisdom on so many issues, may indicate that we are on the brink of a new era of conflict. Finding new, breakthrough ideas to understand and defeat these threats may prove to be the most important challenge we face. ∎

The opinions expressed in this article do not necessarily reflect the views or policies of the U.S. government.

Endnotes

1. See Rupert Smith, *The Utility of Force: The Art of War in the Modern World* (New York: Alfred A. Knopf, 2007), especially pp. 3-28 and 269-335.

2. See Gerald K. Haines and Robert E. Leggett, *Watching the Bear: Essays on CIA's Analysis of the Soviet Union* (Washington, D.C.: Central Intelligence Agency, Center for the Study of Intelligence, 2003), especially chapters VI and VII.

3. See Kevin M. Woods et. al, *Iraqi Perspectives Project: A View of Operation Iraqi Freedom from Saddam's Senior Leadership* (Joint Forces Command, Joint Center for Operational Analysis), p. 92.

4. Intelligence and Security Committee, *Report Into the London Terrorist Attacks on 7 July 2005* (London: The Stationery Office, May 2006), p. 12.

5. See David Kilcullen, "Countering Global Insurgency," *Small Wars Journal* (November 2004) and available at *http://www.smallwarsjournal.com/documents/kilcullen.pdf*; Williamson Murray (ed.), *Strategic Challenges for Counterinsurgency and the Global War on Terrorism* (Carlisle, PA: Strategic Studies Institute, 2006); and Bruce Hoffman, "From War on Terror to Global Counterinsurgency," *Current History* (December 2006): pp. 423-429.

6. Professor Michael Vlahos, Johns Hopkins University Applied Physics Laboratory, personal communication, December 2006.

7. I am indebted to Mr. Steve Eames for this conceptual formulation.

8. Compiled from figures in International Institute for Strategic Studies, *Military Balance 2007*, pp. 15-50.

9. Compiled from U.S. State Department and U.S. Agency for International Development, *Congressional Budget Justification 2007*, table 9.

10. The U.S. Army alone employs well over 5,000 band musicians, according to a March 2007 job advertisement; see *http://bands.army.mil/jobs/default.asp*.

11. Department of Defense, *Quadrennial Defense Review Report* (2 February 2006): pp. 83-91.

12. See Max Boot, Congressional Testimony Before the House Armed Services Committee, 29 June 2006, at *http://www.globalsecurity.org/military/library/congress/2006_hr/060629-boot.pdf*.

13. See Central Intelligence Agency, *The Office of Strategic Services: America's First Intelligence Agency* at *https://www.cia.gov/cia/publications/oss/index.htm*.

14. The seven standard SOF missions are Direct Action (DA), Special Reconnaissance (SR), Unconventional Warfare (UW), Foreign Internal Defence (FID), Counter-Terrorism (CT), Psychological Operations (PSYOP), and Civil Affairs (CA).

A Strategic Assessment of Progress Against the Terrorist Threat

Office of the Coordinator for Counterterrorism
U.S. Department of State

U.S. law requires the secretary of state to annually provide Congress with a full and complete report on terrorism. The following article is taken from the U.S. Department of State's Country Reports on Terrorism 2006, *which was released in April 2007.*

Five years after the attacks of September 11, 2001, the international community's conflict with transnational terrorists continues. Cooperative international efforts have produced genuine security improvements—particularly in securing borders and transportation, enhancing document security, disrupting terrorist financing, and restricting the movement of terrorists. The international community has also achieved significant success in dismantling terrorist organizations and disrupting their leadership. This has contributed to reduced terrorist operational capabilities and the detention or death of numerous key terrorist leaders.

Working with allies and partners across the world, through coordination and information sharing, we have created a less permissive operating environment for terrorists, keeping leaders on the move or in hiding and degrading their ability to plan and mount attacks. Canada, Australia, the United Kingdom, Saudi Arabia, Turkey, Pakistan, Afghanistan, and many other partners played major roles in this success, recognizing that international terrorism represents a threat to the whole international community.

Through the Regional Strategic Initiative, the State Department is working with ambassadors and interagency representatives in key terrorist theaters of operation to assess the threat and devise collaborative strategies, action plans, and policy recommendations. We have made progress in organizing regional responses to terrorists who operate in ungoverned spaces or across national borders. This initiative has produced better intra-governmental coordination among U.S. government agencies, greater cooperation with and between regional partners, and improved strategic planning and prioritization, allowing us to use all tools of statecraft to establish long-term measures to marginalize terrorists.

Continuing Challenges

Despite this undeniable progress, major challenges remain. Several states continue to sponsor terrorism. Iran remains the most significant state sponsor of terrorism and continues to threaten its neighbors and destabilize Iraq by providing weapons, training, advice, and funding to select Iraqi Shia militants. Syria, both directly and in coordination with Hezbollah, has attempted to undermine the elected government of Lebanon and roll back progress toward democratization in the Middle East. Syria also supports some Iraqi Baathists and militants and has continued to allow foreign fighters and terrorists to transit through its borders into Iraq.

International intervention in Iraq has brought measurable benefits. It has removed an abusive totalitarian regime with a history of sponsoring and supporting regional terrorism and has allowed a new democratic political process to emerge. It also, however, has been used by terrorists as a rallying cry for radicalization and extremist activity that has contributed to instability in neighboring countries.

Afghanistan remains threatened by Taliban insurgents and religious extremists, some of whom are linked to al-Qaida and to sponsors outside the country. In Afghanistan, public support for the government remains high, national institutions are getting stronger, and the majority of Afghans believe they are better off than under the Taliban. But to defeat the resurgent threat, the international community must deliver promised assistance and work with Afghans to build counterinsurgency capabilities, ensure legitimate and effective governance, and counter the surge in narcotics cultivation.

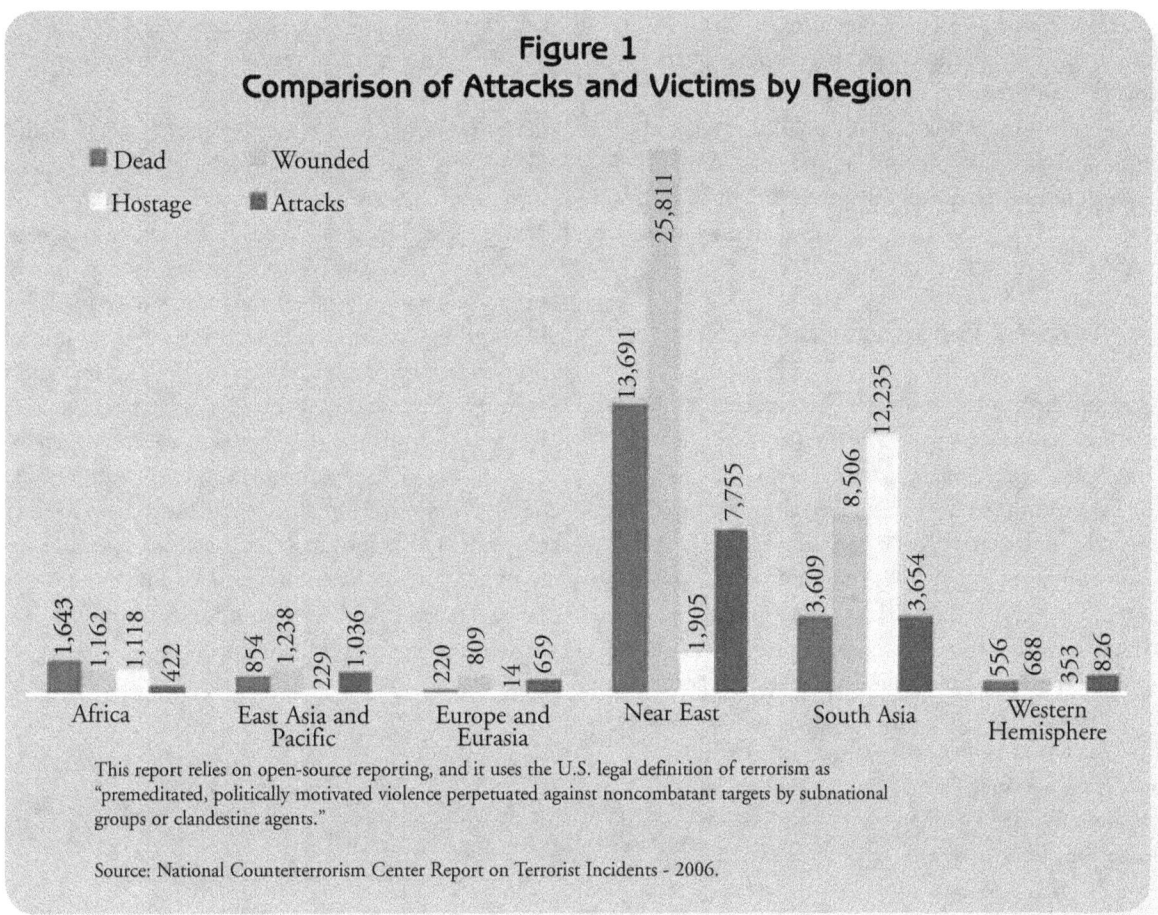

Figure 1
Comparison of Attacks and Victims by Region

Legend: Dead, Wounded, Hostage, Attacks

Africa: 1,643 / 1,162 / 1,118 / 422

East Asia and Pacific: 854 / 1,238 / 229 / 1,036

Europe and Eurasia: 220 / 809 / 14 / 659

Near East: 13,691 / 25,811 / 1,905 / 7,755

South Asia: 3,609 / 8,506 / 12,235 / 3,654

Western Hemisphere: 556 / 688 / 353 / 826

This report relies on open-source reporting, and it uses the U.S. legal definition of terrorism as "premeditated, politically motivated violence perpetuated against noncombatant targets by subnational groups or clandestine agents."

Source: National Counterterrorism Center Report on Terrorist Incidents - 2006.

The Israeli/Palestinian conflict remains a source of terrorist motivation. The holding of free elections in the Palestinian Territories was a welcome sign of democratization, but Hamas' subsequent refusal to disavow terrorism or accept Israel's internationally accepted right to exist undermined the election's impact. Terrorist activity emanating from the Palestinian Territories remains a key destabilizing factor and a cause for concern.

The summer war in Lebanon between Israel and Hezbollah was a prime example of how Hezbollah's continued efforts to manipulate persisting grievances along the Israeli/Lebanese border can quickly escalate into open warfare. The conflict did force the international community again to demand Hezbollah's complete disarmament, in U.N. Security Council Resolution (UNSCR) 1701, and generated a renewed international commitment to support a peaceful, stable, multisectarian democracy in Lebanon. Even so, Hezbollah, a designated foreign terrorist organization, in combination with state sponsors of terrorism Iran and Syria, continues to undermine the elected government of Lebanon and remains a serious security threat in the Middle East.

Al-Qaida and its affiliates have adapted to our success in disrupting their operational capability by focusing more attention and resources on their propaganda and misinformation efforts. They exploit and interpret the actions of numerous local, pseudo-independent actors, using them to mobilize supporters and sympathizers, intimidate opponents, and influence international opinion. Terrorists consider information operations to be a principal part of their effort. The international community has yet to muster a coordinated and effectively resourced counter to extremist propaganda.

Overall, al-Qaida and its loose confederation of affiliated movements remain the most immediate national security threat to the United States and a significant security challenge to the international community.

Key al-Qaida Trends

Single terrorist events, like the Askariya mosque bombing in Samarra, Iraq, on February 22, 2006, which provoked widespread sectarian violence and changed the character of the war in Iraq, can become triggers for broader conflict or templates for copycat attacks. Because terrorism is fundamentally political, the political significance of major events is vital in determining meaningful responses. Thus, the trends presented in this section are interpretive—they provide qualitative insight of statistical details.

Terrorist Propaganda Warfare

As identified in the 2005 *Country Reports*, the international community's success in disrupting terrorist leadership and operational capacity led al-Qaida to focus greater efforts on misinformation and anti-Western propaganda. This trend accelerated this year, with al-Qaida cynically exploiting the grievances of local groups and attempting to portray itself as the vanguard of a global movement. Al-Qaida still retains some operational capability and the intent to mount large-scale spectacular attacks, including on the United States and other high-profile Western targets. Overall, however, al-Qaida's current approach focuses on propaganda warfare—using a combination of terrorist attacks, insurgency, media broadcasts, Internet-based propaganda, and subversion to undermine confidence and unity in Western populations and generate the false perception of a powerful worldwide movement.

The Terrorist "Conveyor Belt"

Radicalization of immigrant populations, youth, and alienated minorities in Europe, the Middle East, and Africa continued. It became increasingly clear, however, that such radicalization does not occur by accident, or because such populations are innately prone to extremism. Rather, there was increasing evidence of terrorists and extremists manipulating the grievances of alienated youth or immigrant populations and then

cynically exploiting those grievances to subvert legitimate authority and create unrest.

Terrorists seek to manipulate grievances in order to radicalize others by pulling them further and further into illegal activities. This is best represented as a "conveyor belt" through which terrorists seek to convert alienated or aggrieved populations, convert them to extremist viewpoints, and turn them, by stages, into sympathizers, supporters, and, ultimately, members of terrorist networks. In some regions, this includes efforts by al-Qaida and other terrorists to exploit insurgency and communal conflict as radicalization and recruitment tools, especially using the Internet to convey their message. Countering such efforts demands that we treat immigrant and youth populations not as a source of threat to be defended against, but as a target of enemy subversion to be protected and supported. It also requires community leaders to take responsibility for the actions of members within their communities and act to counteract extremist subversion.

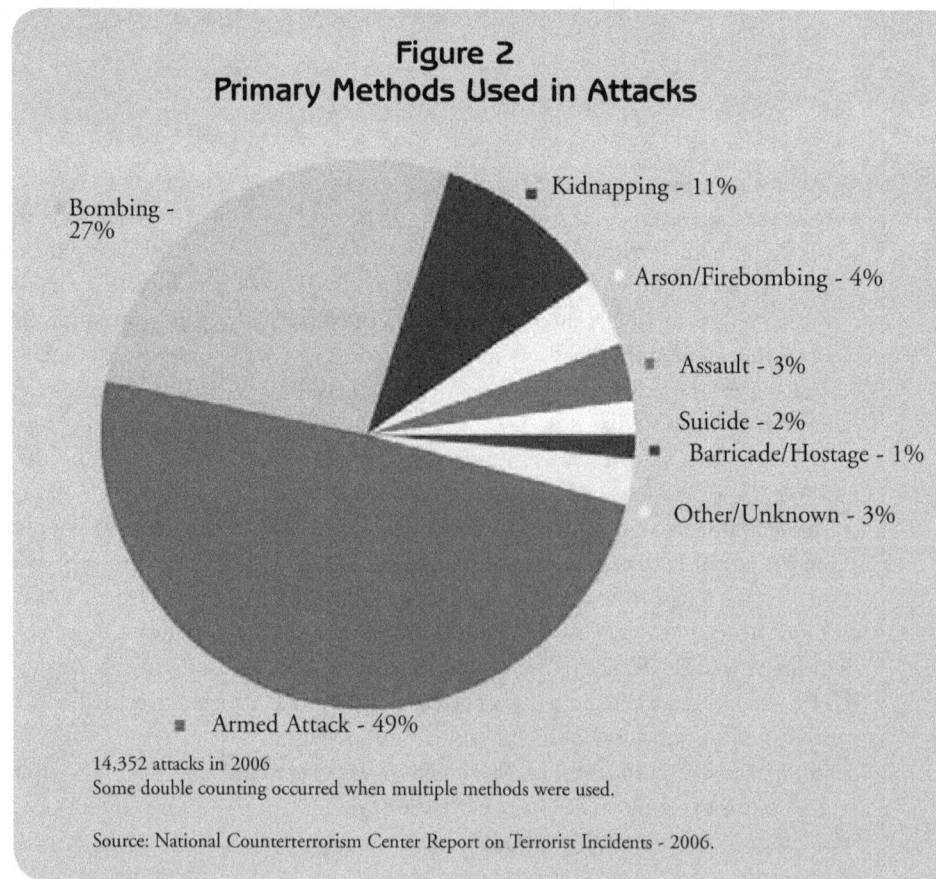

Figure 2
Primary Methods Used in Attacks

Bombing - 27%

Kidnapping - 11%

Arson/Firebombing - 4%

Assault - 3%

Suicide - 2%
Barricade/Hostage - 1%

Other/Unknown - 3%

Armed Attack - 49%

14,352 attacks in 2006
Some double counting occurred when multiple methods were used.

Source: National Counterterrorism Center Report on Terrorist Incidents - 2006.

A New Kind of Enemy

The surface events mentioned above highlight a deeper trend: the transformation of international terrorism from the traditional forms that Congress intended to address when it established the annual *Country Reports* series into a broader, multifarious approach to transnational nonstate warfare that now resembles a form of global insurgency. We have entered a new era of conflict that may demand new paradigms and different responses from those of previous eras.

Al-Qaida and its core leadership group represent a global action network that seeks to aggregate and exploit the effects of widely dispersed, semi-independent actors. It openly describes itself as a transnational guerrilla movement and applies classic insurgent strategies at the global level. Al-Qaida applies terrorism, but also subversion, propaganda, and open warfare, and it seeks weapons of mass destruction in order to inflict the maximum possible damage on its opponents. It links and exploits a wider, more nebulous community of regional, national, and local actors who share some of its objectives, but also pursue their own local agendas. Finally, it works through regional and cross-border safe havens that facilitate its actions while hampering government responses.

Disaggregating the Threat

To the extent that al-Qaida succeeds in aggregating this broader constellation of extremist actors, it can begin to pursue more frequent and geographically extensive terror attacks. Therefore, we must act to disaggregate the threat, through international cooperation, counterpropaganda, counter-subversion, counterinsurgency, and traditional counterterrorism.

Disaggregation breaks the links in the chain that exploit ordinary people's grievances and manipulates them into becoming terrorists. It seeks to provide those who are already radicalized with a way out and to create pathways for alienated groups to redress their legitimate grievances without joining the terrorist network. Disaggregation denies al-Qaida its primary objective of achieving leadership over extremist movements worldwide and unifying them into a single movement. It does not remove the threat but helps reduce it to less dangerous local components that can be dealt with by individual governments and communities working together.

Trusted Networks

Such cooperation requires the creation of trusted networks to displace and marginalize extremist networks. While killing and capturing key terrorist actors is fundamental in combating terrorism, it can have detrimental effects. These actions do not eliminate the threat and, if mishandled, can be actively counterproductive. Instead, we must seek to build trusted networks of governments, private citizens and organizations, multilateral institutions, and business organizations that work collaboratively to defeat the threat from violent extremism.

Such networks, over time, help wean at-risk populations away from subversive manipulation by terrorists and create mechanisms to address people's needs and grievances, thus marginalizing terrorists. Youth organizations, educational networks, business partnerships, women's empowerment, and local development initiatives can all play a role, with government as a supportive partner.

Leaders, Safe Havens, Underlying Conditions

To make such active measures effective, the three strategic components of the terrorist threat that must be neutralized are leaders, safe havens, and underlying conditions. Leaders provide a motivating, mobilizing, and organizing function and act as symbolic figureheads. Safe havens, which are often in ungoverned or undergoverned spaces, provide a secure environment for training, planning, financial, and operational support, and a base for mounting attacks. They may be physical or virtual in nature. In addition, underlying conditions provide the fuel, in the form of grievances and conflicts that power the processes of radicalization.

Treating this new era of conflict as a form of global insurgency implies that counterinsurgency methods are fundamental in combating the new form of transnational terrorism. These methods include, firstly, a focus on protecting and securing the population, and, secondly, politically and physically marginalizing the insurgents, winning the support and cooperation of at-risk populations by targeted political and development measures, and conducting precise intelligence-led special operations to eliminate critical enemy elements with minimal collateral damage.

Integrating All Elements of National Power

All elements of national power, including diplomatic, military, economic, and intelligence, must be integrated and applied in a coordinated whole-of-government fashion. The intellectual and psychological dimensions of the threat are at least as important as its physical dimension, so countermeasures must be adequately coordinated and resourced. Thus, the military component of national power plays only a supporting role in this effort; the primary focus is on nonmilitary influence.

Because the enemy is a nonstate actor who thrives among disaffected populations, private-sector efforts are at least as important as government activity. Citizen diplomacy, cultural activity, person-to-person contact, economic cooperation and development, and the application of media and academic resources are key components of our response to the threat. Motivating, mobilizing, and supporting such privately led activities are key leadership tasks in the new environment.

Commitment—the Key to Success

Experience since 9/11 has shown that the key success factor in confronting violent extremism is the commitment by governments to work with each other, with the international community, with private-sector organizations, and with their citizens and immigrant populations.

Where governments cooperate, build trusted networks, seek active informed support from their people, provide responsive, effective, and legitimate governance, and engage closely with the international community, the threat from terrorism has been significantly reduced.

Where governments have lacked commitment in working with their neighbors and engaging the support of their people, terrorism and the instability and conflict that terrorists exploit remain key sources of threat. ∎

Terrorism in 2006

From the U.S. National Counterterrorism Center's Annex to the 2006 *Country Reports on Terrorism* (numbers are approximate)

14,352	Terrorist attacks worldwide
74,545	Noncombatants killed, injured, or kidnapped
20,570	Civilians killed
1,800	Children killed or injured
430	Students killed or injured
215	Teachers killed or injured
129	Journalists killed or injured
8,200	Police officers killed or injured
1,300	Government leaders, workers, and bodyguards killed or injured
15,855	People kidnapped
Over 50	Percentage of Muslim victims
9,000	Terrorist attacks with unidentified perpetrators
300	Groups identified as connected to remaining attacks
19,500	Schools, businesses, other structures, and vehicles struck
350	Mosques targeted or struck

Bibliography

Additional readings on terrorism

Bin Hassan, Muhammad Haniff. "Key Considerations in Counterideological Work Against Terrorist Ideology." *Studies in Conflict & Terrorism*, vol. 29, no. 6 (September 2006): pp. 561-588.

Bloom, Mia. *Dying to Kill: The Allure of Suicide Terror.* New York: Columbia University Press, 2005.

Borum, Randy. *Psychology of Terrorism.* Tampa, FL: University of South Florida, 2004.

Fouda, Yosri, and Nick Fielding. *Masterminds of Terror: The Truth Behind the Most Devastating Attack the World Has Ever Seen.* Edinburgh, Scotland: Mainstream Publishing, 2003.

Hafez, Mohammed. *Manufacturing Human Bombs: The Making of Palestinian Suicide Bombers.* Washington, D.C.: U.S. Institute of Peace, 2006.

Haqqani, Husain, and Daniel Kimmage. "The Online Bios of Iraq's Suicidology." *The New Republic* (22 September 2005): p. 14.

Hoffman, Bruce. *Inside Terrorism.* New York: Columbia University Press, 2006.

Horgan, John. *The Psychology of Terrorism.* London: Routledge, 2005.

Hronick, Michael S. "Analyzing Terror: Researchers Study the Perpetrators and the Effects of Suicide Terrrorism." *NIJ Journal*, no. 254 (July 2006): pp. 8-11.

Hudson, Rex A. *The Sociology and Psychology of Terrorism: Who Becomes a Terrorist and Why?* Washington, D.C.: Federal Research Division, Library of Congress, 1999.

Kilcullen, David. "Countering Global Insurgency." October 2004. (The long Internet version of a paper subsequently published in the *Journal of Strategic Studies.)*

Laqueur, Walter Z. *No End to War: Terrorism in the Twenty-first Century.* New York: Continuum Books, 2003.

Lelyveld, Joseph. "All Suicide Bombers Are Not Alike." *The New York Times Magazine* (28 October 2001): pp. 48-79.

Martin, Gus. *Understanding Terrorism: Challenges, Perspectives, and Issues.* Thousand Oaks, CA: Sage Publications, Inc., 2006.

Miller, Laurence. "Terrorist Mind: I. A Psychological and Political Analysis." *International Journal of Offender Therapy and Comparative Criminology,* vol. 50, no. 2 (April 2006): pp. 121-138.

Miller, Laurence. "Terrorist Mind: II. Typologies, Psychopathologies, and Practical Guidelines for Investigation." *International Journal of Offender Therapy and Comparative Criminology,* vol. 50, no. 3 (June 2006): pp. 255-268.

Perl, Raphael. "Trends in Terrorism." Washington, D.C.: Congressional Research Service, 2006.

Post, Jerrold M. *Leaders and Their Followers in a Dangerous World: The Psychology of Political Behavior.* Ithaca, NY: Cornell University Press, 2004.

Post, Jerrold M. "When Hatred Is Bred in the Bone: Psycho-cultural Foundations of Contemporary Terrorism." *Political Psychology,* vol. 26, no. 4 (August 2005): pp. 615-636.

Sageman, Marc, *Understanding Terror Networks.* Philadelphia, PA: University of Pennsylvania Press, 2004.

Stern, Jessica. *Terror in the Name of God: Why Religious Militants Kill.* New York: HarperCollins, 2003.

Weimann, Gabriel. *Terror on the Internet: The New Arena, The New Challenges.* Washington, D.C.: United States Institute of Peace, 2006.

Internet Resources

Online resources for terrorism information

U.S. GOVERNMENT

U.S. Air National Guard: Conflict 21's Center for Psychology of Terrorism Studies
http://c21.maxwell.af.mil/cts-ref.htm
The center identifies innovative ideas for research, leveraging of resources, and institutional changes needed to meet the challenges of homeland security and to combat terrorism.

U.S. Congress. Hearing on the Terrorist/Jihadist Use of the Internet for Strategic Communications
http://intelligence.house.gov/Reports.aspx?Section=134
This hearing demonstrates how jihadists effectively use the Internet to communicate with disaffected or young moderate Muslims.

U.S. Department of State: Counterterrorism Office (S/CT)
http://www.state.gov/s/ct/
This office leads a worldwide effort to combat terrorism using all the instruments of statecraft: diplomacy, economic power, intelligence, law enforcement, and military. S/CT provides foreign policy oversight and direction to all U.S. government international counterterrorism activities and is guided by the National Security Strategy and the National Strategy for Combating Terrorism.

Country Reports on Terrorism 2006
A major annual report from the U.S. Department of State Counterterrorism Office.
http://www.state.gov/s/ct/rls/crt/2006/

U.S. Department of State: International Information Programs: International Security: Response to Terrorism
http://usinfo.state.gov/topical/pol/terror/
This site links to news, electronic journals, photos, video segments, documents, fact sheets, and other electronic resources.

U.S. National Defense University: Military Policy Awareness Links—Terrorism: Terrorist Group Profiles
http://merln.ndu.edu/index.cfm?secID=149&pageID=3&type=section#profiles
A group of links from the National Defense University that includes government and think-tank reports on terrorist leaders, ideology, and motivations.

U.S. ORGANIZATIONS

Center for Interdisciplinary Policy, Education, and Research on Terrorism (CIPERT)
http://www.cipert.org/
CIPERT'S mission is to promote the scientific understanding of the causes and effects of political violence, especially terrorism, and to translate this understanding into effective policy, education, and research.

Counterterrorism Blog
http://counterterrorismblog.org/
This Web log features posts from former law enforcement officials and congressional staffers, as well as links to news stories and research reports.

Public Broadcasting System: Frontline—The Roots of Terror (Teacher's Guide)
http://www.pbs.org/wgbh/pages/frontline/teach/terror/
This seminal television program produced a series of documentaries, all of which dealt with the roots of terrorism and the complex evolution of U.S. policy and Islamic fundamentalism. *Frontline* also developed an in-depth teachers' guide for use with the programs to meet a variety of instructional needs and to help students explore these intricate issues.

Terrorism Knowledge Base
http://www.tkb.org
The Terrorism Knowledge Base, a collaboration of government, nongovernmental organizations, and think tanks, covers the history, affiliations, locations, and tactics of terrorist groups operating across the world, with more than 35 years of terrorism incident data and hundreds of group and leader profiles and trials.

ACADEMIC ORGANIZATIONS

America's War Against Terrorism: Psychological Causes of Terrorism

http://www.lib.umich.edu/govdocs/usterror.html#psychter
The University of Michigan's mega Internet documents center provides U.S. foreign policy and government information about America's war against terrorism and its aftermath.

Kennedy School of Government: Undermining Terrorism

http://www.ksg.harvard.edu/terrorism/
This portal captures key academic papers, reports, books, op-eds, and conferences on undermining terrorism.

The National Center on the Psychology of Terrorism (NCPT)

http://www.terrorismpsychology.org/Default.aspx?tabid=1
This center argues that psychology and psychological science is critical to understanding terrorism and to combating its consequences. It will join forces with CIPERT in the future.

National Consortium for the Study of Terrorism and Responses to Terrorism (START)

http://www.start.umd.edu
Based at the University of Maryland, START is tasked by the Department of Homeland Security's Science and Technology Directorate with using data from the social and behavioral sciences to improve understanding of the origins, dynamics, and social and psychological impacts of terrorism.

INTERNATIONAL ORGANIZATIONS

Center for Defense Information (CDI): Terrorism Project

http://www.cdi.org/program/issue/index.cfm?ProgramID=39&issueid=138
CDI's Terrorism Project is designed to provide insights, in-depth analysis, and facts on the military, security, and foreign policy challenges of terrorism.

Institute for Counter-Terrorism

http://www.ict.org.il/
This think tank provides detailed profiles of terrorist organizations and brief reports on terrorist-related activities.

International Center for the Study of Terrorism

http://www.wun.ac.uk/ctcenter/
The center is built around a core of universities that use theories, methods, findings, and perspectives from a wide range of disciplines, including psychology and sociology, and apply them to studying terrorism and to developing effective means of responding to the threat of terrorism.

Middle East Media Research Institute: Islamist Websites Monitor Project

http://memri.org/iwmp.html
The Islamist Websites Monitor, which focuses on the major jihadi Web sites, will be regularly releasing translated news, analysis, and videos from these sites

---

The U.S. Department of State assumes no responsibility for the content and availability of the resources from other agencies and organizations listed above. All Internet links were active as of May 2007.

www.ingramcontent.com/pod-product-compliance
Lightning Source LLC
Chambersburg PA
CBHW080609290526
45790CB00007B/2701